OBTAINING PATENTS

Second Edition

Martin P.J. Kratz

CARSWELL
Thomson Professional Publishing

The paper used in this publication meets the minimum requirements of American National Standard for Information Sciences — Permanence of Paper for Printed Library Materials, ANSI Z39.48-1984.

Canadian Cataloguing in Publication Data

Kratz, Martin P.J.
    Obtaining patents

(Canada practice guide. Intellectual property)
2nd ed.
Includes index.
ISBN 0-459-26253-X

1. Patent practice – Canada.   2. Patent laws and
legislation – Canada.
I. Title.   II. Series.

KE2929.K73 1999   346.7104'86   C99-932045-9
KF3120.K73 1999

CARSWELL
Thomson Professional Publishing

One Corporate Plaza, 2075 Kennedy Road, Scarborough, Ontario M1T 3V4
Customer Relations:
Toronto 1-416-609-3800
Elsewhere in Canada/U.S. 1-800-387-5164
Fax: 1-416-298-5094

Table of Contents

Chapter 1
FIRST CONTACT WITH THE CLIENT

Chapter 4
PREPARATION

Chapter 5
TAKING ACTION

Chapter 6
CLOSING THE FILE

APPENDICES

ACKNOWLEDGMENTS

I acknowledge the support and encouragement of my wife, Christina, who gave me the time to finish the project. Alexandra and Marcus were patient and made few interruptions. Particularly, I thank Ms. Roseann Caldwell, Patent Agent, Bennett Jones for her review of early manuscripts and helpful comments and suggestions.

INTRODUCTION

SCOPE OF THE BOOK

- This book is aimed at the general practitioner acting as advisor to an inventor.

- It is hoped that the reader will obtain a number of benefits from this book including:

  ° being more knowledgeable about the patent filing process;

  ° having a better appreciation of basic patent law issues and hence be able to assist in making better business and legal decisions during the filing and prosecution of the application;

  ° being able to provide more knowledgeable and therefore better communication with a patent agent and be better able to intelligently and actively manage the work done by a patent agent.

- This book is not a substitute for the use of a registered patent agent in making an application for a patent.

- The field of patent law is very complex and patent rights may be very significant. This text is introductory in scope and provides the basic framework for the patent system in Canada. There are many rules, practices and procedures outside the scope of this text. *You may wish to consult one or more of the sources listed in Appendix N. You may also wish to consult with a lawyer knowledgeable in the field of patent law for specific legal advice relating to your client's particular situation.*

GLOSSARY OF TERMS

author:	the creator of a thing protected by copyright
claim:	the description of the elements of the invention and which set out the scope and limits of the patentee's rights
designer:	the creator of an industrial design (or design)
work:	a thing protectable under copyright law
invention:	a thing or process which may be patentable
inventor:	the creator of an invention
patentee:	the owner of the patent
pirate:	an infringer
prosecute:	to seek to resolve issues arising from an application raised by the official or examiner in the applicable registry
office action:	an official letter from the patent examiner arising from a substantive review of the patent application

- The text will be updated periodically to address changes in law and practice. If you have any suggestions please send them to me at either: kratzm@bennetjones.ca on the Internet; or 4500 Bankers Hall East, 855-2nd Street S.W., Calgary, Alberta, T2P 4K7, (403) 298-3650, FAX (403) 265-7219.

1

FIRST CONTACT WITH THE CLIENT

1.1 CHARACTERIZATION OF THE TECHNOLOGY

- A critical early step is to properly characterize the work, device, process or thing (referred to informally as the "technology" in this chapter) the client wants to protect. *The client may know nothing about patents and may need copyright, industrial design, trade-mark or other protection or a combination of these.*

1.2 SPECIAL ISSUES

- Be prepared to immediately address the status of disclosures of the invention. (*See Chapters 2 and 3 for more deTailed information.*)

- In order to minimize the risk of any (further) disclosures you may wish to provide the client with a form of non-disclosure agreement. Several examples are attached in Appendices K and L. A checklist on typical terms in a non-disclosure agreement is attached in Appendix M. You will need to develop or adapt documents to meet your client's particular requirements. *The purpose of non-disclosure agreements are to seek to establish obligations of secrecy with other persons who may be provided access to the invention. While such obligations may, in certain cases, arise out of a relationship or the circumstances, the use of the non-disclosure agreement provides clear evidence of the establishment of a relationship of confidence and sets out the terms and any limits of that relationship.*

1.3 FORMS OF INTELLECTUAL PROPERTY

In order to be as complete as possible you should review the potential applicability of each form of intellectual property protection to the client's technology. For more details on the following types of intellectual property consult the resources identified in Appendix N or review *Canadian Intellectual Property Law* (Toronto: Carswell, 1998). Note that overlapping protection is likely in many cases. (*The examples at the end of the chapter may assist you, but please note the cautions regarding them.*)

1.3.1 TRADE-MARKS

In Canada, the traditional theory is that trade-marks serve to identify the "source" of the products or services associated with the trade-mark. Given the growth of licensing and franchise operations, the role of trade-marks is increasingly evolving to distinguish one trader's product or service from that of another trader.

- A trade-mark is a way of distinguishing one trader's product or service from that of another trader.

- Trade-marks protect the goodwill and reputation associated with a product or service.

- A trade-mark may be any form of indication or sign, such as:

  ° a word (*i.e.*, "IBM");

  ° a phrase or slogan (also known as "word marks") (*i.e.*, "Mr. Christie, You Make Good Cookies");

  ° a logo or design (also known as a "design mark") (*i.e.*, the McDonald's double arches); or

  ° a distinctive shape (also known as a "distinguishing guise") (*i.e.*, the unique shape of the Coca Cola bottle).

- *Some jurisdictions also provide protection for other indicators such as a specific sound or smell associated with a product or service.*

- Trade-mark law provides essentially no protection for the design of the technology, product or service except that certain well-known shapes may be protected as distinguishing guises.

- Unlike copyright, where rights arise on creation, or patent and industrial design, where rights arise on registration, trade-mark rights arise based on the *use* of the trade-mark in association with a product or service.

- Trade-marks may be registered under the provisions of the *Trade-marks Act*, R.S.C. 1985, c. T-13, as amended. (Discussion on the nature of trade-mark rights, details on making a trade-mark application, proper trade-mark use and enforcement of trade-mark rights may be found in Donna G. White, *Selecting and Protecting Trade-Marks 1995*, Canada Practice Guide (Toronto: Carswell, 1994)).

(a) Copyright and Trade-Marks

Unlike the complications of the relationship between copyright and industrial design law or the lesser complications of copyright and patent law, the provisions of Canada's copyright law and trade-mark law co-exist and complement each other in a useful manner.

Many traders use artistic works, such as designs, logos or distinguishing guises, as design marks to distinguish their wares and services from those of others. Such artistic works may be protected under copyright law. As a result, it may be possible for the trade-mark owner to take action in respect of infringement or other unfair competition by bringing both trade-mark infringement action and copyright infringement action.

- A trade-mark only provides protection in relation to specific uses, while a copyright provides protection in relation to any substantially similar copy, largely regardless of use.

- As far as possible the trade-mark agent or advisor carrying out the registration of the trade-marks should seek to address the issue of protection of the copyright in design marks. (For more details on copyright issues, see Martin P.J. Kratz, *Protecting Copyright and Industrial Design Second Edition*, Canada Practice Guide (Toronto: Carswell, 1999)).

(b) Industrial Design and Trade-Marks

- In some cases distinctive shapes which may be considered for trade-mark protection as distinguishing guises may also qualify for protection under the industrial design system. In such a case, the owner should consider seeking to obtain, if still possible, industrial design protection for the unique design. *Note there is only one year from any making public of the design or shape in which to seek industrial design protection.*

- As far as possible the trade-mark agent or advisor carrying out the registration of the trade-marks should seek to address the issue of protection of any industrial design rights in a distinguishing guise. (For more details on industrial design issues, see *Protecting Copyright and Industrial Design Second Edition*.)

1.3.2 PATENTS

- Patents protect inventions. (*For more details on the nature of patents, see Chapter 2.*)

- To be an invention, a design, technology or advance must satisfy strict requirements of novelty, inventive merit and utility.

- An invention may be:

    ° a product (*i.e.*, a better mousetrap);

    ° a process (*i.e.*, a way of doing something, a unique set of logically inter-related steps to do something);

    ° a composition (*i.e.*, a unique combination of different elements); or

    ° an apparatus (*i.e.*, a unique machine or device).

- In each case, the invention must be new. It cannot be something that has been available in the marketplace for many years. (*See section 2.6.3, below, for discussion of novelty.*)

- An invention must be useful. It must solve a practical problem. (*See section 2.6.2, below, for discussion of utility.*)

- An invention must also show inventive merit. It must be an unexpected or non-obvious solution to the problem. (*See section 2.6.4, below, for discussion of inventive merit.*)

- Unlike copyright but similar to industrial design, the patent system requires registration in a country in order to create enforceable rights within that country.

- Unlike copyright or industrial design, a patent protects useful features of a technology, work or a design.

- A 20-year term of protection is available in Canada. The term is measured from the date of application for the patent.

- The rules on novelty and the requirement of inventive merit (or non-obviousness) are complex.

- *Failure to file an application prior to any public use, disclosure or sale of the invention or a product or process em- bodying the invention may result in loss of rights! If you are unsure on this point, discuss the particular facts with an intellectual property lawyer.*

1.3.3 TRADE SECRET LAW

- Information, data, ideas, designs or concepts may be protected under trade secret law.

- This system of law arose from the common law and requires:

  ° an obligation of confidence (*i.e.*, an obligation to keep the information secret);

7

- ° the subject-matter itself must be confidential (*i.e.*, it must be secret, not publicly known); and

- ° disclosure of the information must result in actual or threatened detriment to the holder of the information.

- The obligation of confidence may arise expressly, such as under a non-disclosure agreement or as a term in a contract, or by implication or conduct (*i.e.*, if confidential information was disclosed in circumstances in which the parties ought to know the information was imparted in confidence). See, for example, *Cadbury Schweppes Inc. v. FBI Foods Ltd.* (1999), 167 D.L.R. (4th) 577 (S.C.C.), *International Corona Resources Ltd. v. Lac Minerals Ltd.* (1989), 26 C.P.R. (3d) 97, 44 B.L.R. 1 (S.C.C.); *Seager v. Copydex Ltd.*,(1967) 2 All E.R. 415 (Eng. C.A.).

- *Examples of non-disclosure agreements are shown in Appendices K and L and a checklist of terms in such agreements is shown in Appendix M.*

- The requirement of an obligation of confidence means that the disclosing party must have a relationship with the receiving party. No obligations arise with strangers. *This is an important limit on the protection available under trade secret law.*

- The second requirement, that the subject-matter must be secret, means that the information cannot have been made available to the public.

- Examples of disclosures which would preclude protection include:

  - ° publication of the information in an article or brochure;

  - ° public use;

  - ° sale of a product embodying the information or from which the information may be extracted; or

- ° filing a patent application which may be laid open to the public 18 months after first filing and obtaining an industrial design registration. (*These last two points are important to note.*)

- *Including information in an application for industrial design or patent protection may result in loss of ability to protect that information under trade secret law.*

- Copyright may co-exist with trade secret protection (see section 63, *Copyright Act*).

- Generally it is not difficult to establish detriment from actual or threatened unauthorized disclosure since such activity results in loss of exclusivity of and control over the information.

- Confidential information may be protected for as long as the information is maintained as secret.

- In certain cases, your client may be able to and wish to utilize a trade secret exception to the *Access to Information Act (Canada)*, R.S.C. 1985, c. A-1, as amended.

1.3.4 COPYRIGHT LAW

- Copyright co-exists with trade secret law and provides very useful rights to compliment the rights under a trade-mark registration.

- Copyright protects the form in which literary, artistic, musical and dramatic works may be expressed and provides a bundle of enforceable rights to the copyright owner. Unlike patent or industrial design law, copyright arises automatically upon the creation of an original work that is fixed in a tangible form. Unlike a trade-mark, which only provides protection in relation to specific uses, copyright provides protection in relation to any substantially similar copy, regardless of use.

- It has been suggested that copyright does not extend to drawings in patent specifications (*Rucker Co. v. Gavel's Vul-*

9

canizing Ltd. (1985), 7 C.P.R. (3d) 294 (Fed. T.D.), varied (1987), 14 C.P.R. (3d) 439 (Fed. T.D.)).

- For most cases and situations the copyright subsists for the life of the author plus the end of the year in which the author dies, plus 50 years. For further information on the nature of copyright and how to protect and enforce rights, see *Protecting Copyright and Industrial Design Second Edition.*

- For unique problems associated with the Internet see Gahtan, Kratz, Mann, *Internet Law* (Toronto: Carswell, 1998).

1.3.5 AUTHOR'S MORAL RIGHTS

- The *Copyright Act* provides for specific moral rights of the author, to permit the author of a work to:

  ° assert paternity of the work or require the author's name to be associated with the work if reasonable in the circumstances (see section 14.1, *Copyright Act*); and

  ° object to or restrain certain uses of or associations with a work (see section 28.2, *Copyright Act*); or

  ° object to or restrain any distortion, mutilations or modification of a work which may be to the prejudice of the honour and reputation of the author (see section 28.2, *Copyright Act*).

- Unlike copyright, the moral rights may not be assigned by the author (see section 14.1(2), *Copyright Act*), however, the author may, expressly or by implication, waive his or her moral rights (see section 14.1(2), *Copyright Act*). Moral rights subsist for the life of the author, plus the end of the year in which the author dies, plus 50 years (section 14.1(2), *Copyright Act*).

- In many cases it may be important that the owner of a technology to which any copyright might apply obtain a waiver of these moral rights so as to ensure they have unfettered use of the technology.

- In any case where:

  ° the true author may not be named;

  ° there may be subsequent modifications or adjustments may need to be made to a work or design; or

  ° where the work (*i.e.*, a design mark) may be used in association with a business, cause, institution,

  it is important to review the possible applicability of any moral rights claims.

1.3.6 INDUSTRIAL DESIGNS

- Industrial design registration is available to protect aesthetic features of an article or product. Notionally, it is intended to provide protection for features of shape, configuration and ornament applied to an article or product.

- Unlike copyright but similar to patents, the industrial design system requires registration in each country in order to create enforceable rights. Registration is for a term of ten years (or for designs before January 1, 1994, five years and the registration was able to be renewed for a further term of five years).

- Unlike patents, industrial designs do not protect any useful features or methods of construction.

- Works which may be the subject of industrial design applications may also be artistic works normally protected by copyright.

- The interrelationship between the *Copyright Act* and *Industrial Design Act* and their respective regulations is very complex. (See *Protecting Copyright and Industrial Design Second Edition* for more details.)

- *Failure to file an application within one year of any public use, disclosure or sale of the design or a product or process bearing the design may result in loss of rights.*

1.3.7 INTEGRATED CIRCUIT TOPOGRAPHIES

The *Integrated Circuit Topography Act,* S.C. 1990, c. 37, as amended, addresses itself to the protection of new integrated circuit designs (called "topographies") and products incorporating those designs. Protection is only available by registering the topographies. The Act provides a registration system with a ten-year term of protection and a number of very significant exemptions allowing use for educational, research purposes and reverse engineering in certain circumstances.

- *Failure to file an application within two years of any commercial sale of a product using the topography may result in loss of rights.*

1.3.8 PLANT BREEDERS' RIGHTS

The *Plant Breeders' Rights Act*, S.C. 1990, c. 20, as amended, provides a system for protection of new crop varieties. Under this system the breeder of a distinct plant variety may obtain a limited monopoly over the production and sale of the reproductive material (*i.e.,* seeds). The breeder may also be able to denominate (*i.e.*, name) the new crop variety.

- The term of protection is 18 years from the issue of the registration of the rights. *Failure to make a timely application may result in loss of rights.*

- Examples of potentially protected plants may be a line, clone, hybrid or genetic variation of a plant. To be registrable the new variety must be stable, uniform and distinct.

- To be capable of protection the new plant variety may not have been sold in Canada prior to filing of the application for registration of the rights. The Act has special provisions dealing with recently prescribed categories and prescribed exemptions (see section 7, *Plant Breeders' Rights Act.*)

- The patentability of life forms is uncertain under Canadian law. (See *Pioneer Hi-Bred Ltd. v. Canada (Commissioner of*

*Patents) (1989), 25 C.I.P.R. 1 (S.C.C.), Harvard College v.
Canada (Commissioner of Patents) (1998), 79 C.P.R. (3d) 98
(Fed. T.D.).)*

1.4 INFORMATION TO OBTAIN IN THE INITIAL INTERVIEW

- Initial information you will need to obtain from your client includes:

  1. **name**
  2. **address**
  3. **citizenship, country of ordinary residence and date of birth**
  4. **occupation and employer information**
  5. **telephone numbers at home and work (*ask if you can call your client at work*)**
  6. **fax number(s)**
  7. **e-mail address**
  8. **billing information.**

- In order to properly characterize the technology your client wants to protect it is important to get as much information from him or her as possible. At this early stage you need to assess all of the elements or components of the technology so that you can determine what form or forms of protection may be applicable.

- Let your client tell his or her story. If necessary, ask probing questions, using simple language, to draw out your client.

- Prepare complete notes of the information provided to you and date them.

1.4.1 DESCRIPTION OF THE TECHNOLOGY

- Obtain as complete a description as possible.

- Confirm your understanding of your client's narrative with such questions as:

  ° How does it work?

13

° How is it to be manufactured/assembled?

° What pre-existing parts are included?

° How is it to be presented to the market?

° What are its useful features?

° What features appeal to the eye?

° Did you make it?

° How did you come to make it?

° Why did you make it?

° How is it different (better) from what already is available?

° Has it been shown/sold/offered for sale/published? (*See Chapter 3 as to disclosure issues and publication bars.*)

- Have your client bring in the technology or go to the client's site to see it.

1.4.2 SEARCH RESULTS

- If your client has carried out any searches, obtain a copy of the search results and search request.

- Caution your client on the limitations of searches (*see section 4.1.3, below*).

1.4.3 INVENTORSHIP INFORMATION

- It is important that you let your client tell you about his or her role in making (or copying) the technology. This will assist in determining if he or she has any claim in it and if there are any infringement problems or issues.

- Ask your client such probing questions as:

  ° What role did you have in making the technology?

  ° Had you seen it before?

  ° Did others help make it? If so, how and what was their contribution?

  ° Did you adapt something already available? If so, in what way?

1.4.4 OWNERSHIP INFORMATION

- In addition to determining if your client has a claim as inventor or author, it is important to identify whether any third party might have an ownership or other interest or claim.

(a) Obligations to Employers

- Obtain details of the client's present employment including:

  ° employer identification;

  ° job description, responsibilities and length of employment;

  ° obtain a copy of all employment and related agreements (*note especially all obligations of confidence/secrecy, obligations to assign inventions, etc., restrictive covenants and other special terms*);

  ° your client's and other's past experience in making any technology at work;

  ° the extent to which the technology relates directly or indirectly to the employer's business;

  ° any use of the employer's tools or resources in making the technology;

    ° any use of or incorporation of confidential information of the employer;

    ° the extent to which the technology was made at work or after hours;

    ° your client's professional and technical training and experience (*i.e.*, is the client an engineer or scientist?);

    ° any special practices in the industry.

(b) Obligations to Partners, Others

- Obtain details of your client's commitments to others such as partners, contractors, financiers, *etc.*

- Identify every person involved in making the technology and obtain a description of their contribution and role.

- Obtain a copy of any agreements with any party regarding the technology.

- Ascertain whether consultants, specialists or experts were used for different parts of the project and the terms under which they made a contribution.

- Ensure your client tells you about the entire development history (including failed prototypes, early experiments, previous versions, *etc.*).

- Identify all contributions, interests and claims of any parties.

- Identify any other sources of the inventive concepts or ideas.

1.4.5 DESCRIPTION OF PRIOR ART

- Ask your client to describe the machines, processes or products which already exist in the field of the technology. In each case, ask your client to identify how his or her technology is better. Examples of how your client's technology may be better might include:

° lower cost to use;

° lower cost to make;

° no/less side effects in use;

° easier to use;

° increased safety in use or manufacture;

° less complex, simpler to maintain, repair;

° more effective in performing the desired functions;

° more completely solves the problem;

° portable/more mobile in use.

- *The specific advantages of your client's technology will depend on the specific circumstances of the technology and the problem being solved. It may be helpful for you and your client to brainstorm on any advantages together. Be sure to write down and date all of the advantages you or your client identify!*

1.4.6 PUBLIC USE, DISCLOSURE OR ACCESS

Your client may have a duty of full disclosure to the Patent Office. It is important to seek to gather as complete information as possible. In each case obtain specific details including dates and places where disclosed, the extent of disclosure and, if possible, copies of the documents, materials or publications disclosed or otherwise made available to the public.

- Have your client describe every occasion of any disclosure or use of the technology including:

   ° any sales of the technology or products made from it;

   ° any sales of other technology or products relating to the technology either from the client's business or from any other person, firm or corporation's business;

    ° any offer for sale of the technology or products made from it;

    ° any product announcements;

    ° any use of the technology or products made from it in public;

    ° any display at trade shows, inventor fairs, *etc.*;

    ° any display or description on a website, discussion in any chatroom or on Usenet or other dissemination on the Internet;

    ° any use of the technology or products made from it in such a way that the elements (or components) of the technology were made available to the public;

    ° any publication of the technology or of any elements or features of it, whether formal or not;

    ° any lecture, seminar or demonstration of the technology or of any elements or features of it;

    ° any applications for government assistance, funding, *etc.*, disclosing the technology or any aspect of it;

    ° any articles in newspapers, journals, trade magazines, *etc.*, which describe the technology or any aspect of it;

    ° any relevant work or technology of co-workers.

- *Review the cautions in Chapter 3.*

- *Rights may be dependent on whether or not disentitling disclosures occurred.*

1.4.7 MARKET PLAN OR STRATEGY

- A client's business and market plans or strategy may give you additional insight into the issues of disclosure, and features of the technology, and may assist you in determining important additional information such as:

° What entity is anticipated to own the technology? *Is a new incorporation necessary?*

° Who will participate in the commercial exploitation of the technology and how? *What agreements are needed?*

° How will the business be financed? *What is the market for the technology? Where is that market? What agreements are necessary? How will your account be paid?*

° What future disclosures are contemplated and when? *Is there a need for a non-disclosure agreement?*

1.5 FINANCIAL REVIEW

• After you have characterized the technology, have obtained details concerning the technology and have determined that there may be some prospect for a patent application (or at least further study of the situation appears warranted) the client will need some idea of the costs to proceed. Ensure the following costs are up to date, add your own fees and disbursements and confirm or revise the costs to use a patent agent.

1.5.1 COSTS TO SEARCH

• *See section 4.1, below, for a more complete list of different types of searches and cautions on the use and limitations of searches.*

• A patentability search is often conducted to review the possibile novelty of an invention. Note that this type of search will not typically identify possible infringement of third party rights. *See section 4.1 for a discussion of infringement searches.*

• Database Search — Cost: From $100 to $300 or more per hour for connect time only. You must also add any fees charged by the searcher and the costs for copies of documents ordered. (*See section 4.1.1, below, for a list of some databases one may search.*)

- Physical Search — U.S. Patent and Trademark Office — Cost: $200 to $1,500 U.S., for limited patentability searches, or more depending on how extensive and comprehensive a search is required.

- Physical Search — Canadian Patent Office — Cost: $200 to $1,500, for limited patentability searches, or more depending on how extensive and comprehensive a search is required.

- Add the costs to review the search results and, as applicable, obtain an opinion regarding the search results. *You may wish to have a patent agent provide that opinion.*

- Add your own fees and disbursements.

- Searches are not required prior to filing an application.

- If your client wishes to file a patent application without carrying out preliminary searches he or she should be made aware that prior patents may exist which already claim the client's technology or important elements of it. This may put the client's investment in preparing the application at risk and also raises the spectre of possible infringement by the client of third-party rights.

1.5.2 COSTS TO FILE

There are a number of costs involved in filing an application (other than your fees and disbursements). These costs include the filing fees, costs for formal drawings, costs for any searches and the patent agent's fees and disbursements, which may be quite substantial (see Chapter 4 as to the role of the patent agent). Formal drawings must usually be prepared by a draftsman, at a cost of $400 to $1,500, generally. The cost of drawings may be deferred by filing informal drawings and awaiting the patent examiner's action.

The preparation of a patent application is a creative art. Often the more time available to prepare the application and the more time spent brainstorming between the inventor and the patent agent will directly affect the scope of the claims and the potential

enforceability of any patent which may issue. While it is impossible to provide any meaningful guidance on a hypothetical patent application a rule of thumb may be a cost of
$5,000 for fees merely to prepare and fix the application for an average invention with an
average degree of co-operation and disclosure from the inventor.

- Some factors which tend to *increase* the patent agent's cost
  are:

  ° complexity of the invention;

  ° degree of interaction with the inventor or others;

  ° difficulties in working with the inventor such as lack of can-
    dour, lack of full disclosure, difficulty in expressing himself
    or herself in an organized fashion, difficulty in communi-
    cating in writing;

  ° complex co-inventorship issues;

  ° inadequacy of the inventor's disclosure; and

  ° lack of preliminary searches.

- Some factors which tend to *decrease* the patent agent's
  cost are:

  ° simplicity of the invention;

  ° highly co-operative inventor who is completely candid,
    able to communicate in an organized manner, and able to
    communicate effectively in writing;

  ° complete and detailed disclosure; and

  ° meaningful preliminary searches.

- The fees charged by the Patent Office include:

  ° filing fee
    if a small entity — $150
    otherwise — $300

  ° request for examination
    if a small entity — $200
    otherwise — $400

- *For other fees and charges, see Appendix G.*

1.5.3 COSTS TO PROSECUTE

The cost to prosecute the application consists of the patent agent's fees and disbursements in evaluating the examiner's office action, working with the inventor in developing a response and responding to the examiner. This may be an iterative process. The patent agent's costs will depend on the work done by both you and the inventor, the effectiveness and completeness of your communications and the actions of the Patent Office examiner.

- Some of the costs and fees which may arise during this stage are the drafting expenses, as well as:

  ° completion of an application not complete on its filing date — $200

  ° maintenance fees (due even during the application stage) — see section 1.5.4, below

- The same factors that influence costs during the application stage also apply in prosecuting the application.

1.5.4 COSTS TO MAINTAIN PATENT

- If the patent application is allowed, additional costs may arise, including the patent agent's fees and:

  ° for grant of a patent
       if a small entity — $150
       otherwise — $300
       plus $4 per page for specifications and drawings over 100 pages)

  ° annual maintenance fees
       if a small entity — $50 to
                                   $200*
       otherwise — $100 to $400*

---

* Maintenance fees increase during the term of the application/patent. For details see Appendix G. See also Rule 99, Patent Rules.

° publication of a
  licence notice — $20

1.5.5 INTERNATIONAL FILINGS

- The costs to file and prosecute a patent application vary from country to country, but you should estimate fees of at least $10,000 per patent per country for the average invention. Higher costs will arise in countries where translations must also be filed. *Note that foreign filing costs will be incurred in foreign currency, thus currency fluctuations can add to the difficulty of estimating costs.*

- Factors which tend to increase these costs are the same as set out in section 1.5.2, above. In addition, translation costs and the fees and charges levied by the particular jurisdiction should be considered.

- Factors which tend to decrease these costs are the same as set out in section 1.5.2, above. In addition, in some cases filings may be carried out in the same language and the use of certain treaties (such as the European Patent Treaty) may reduce per country filing costs in certain circumstances.

- International filings require:

  ° a review of the treaty status of each country;
  ° a review of each country's domestic law; and
  ° a consideration of any factors (*i.e.*, public use, disclosure, *etc.*) which may disentitle the applicant to protection.

1.6 THE BUSINESS DECISION

While the rights which may potentially be obtained under an issued patent may be significant, the costs to file, prosecute and obtain patent protection are a considerable investment for many inventors. In addition, the inventor bears the burden of bringing enforcement action against infringers. Moreover, a patent may not issue despite the considerable costs and efforts to make the application. In some cases patent rights may provide substantial rights and may provide a sound basis for a business, or the patent may relate to a very specific improvement of prior technology.

- You should seek to have your client address the business issues surrounding the filing of a patent application, as only he or she can assess the potential scope of protection against the costs and the risk that no patent may ever issue.

- *Your role is to provide the legal framework for this decision, not to make the business decision. In properly performing your role you are assisting the client with his or her business decision and you are providing a valuable service.*

1.7   INSTRUCTIONS TO PROCEED

- Confirm your client's instructions in writing, whether or not you have been asked to proceed.

1.7.1 EXAMPLES OF CHARACTERIZATION OF TECHNOLOGY

- The following examples may assist in how you might seek to characterize a product, process, thing or device and determine what forms of intellectual property protection might be applicable.

- *Appreciate that in the particular circumstances some of the areas of law may not be applicable (for example, the design or process may not be an invention and therefore not patentable).*

- By going through a comprehensive analysis of the device and related materials you are most likely to identify any potential intellectual property issues. *Note that your client may impair your ability to carry out a complete or comprehensive review by not giving you access to all the relevant information or, in some cases, by misleading you as to the origin or source of some of the creative contributions.*

(a) Example One

- Your client comes to your office and shows you a device he or she has created. It is an electronic gadget. The device comes in a case. Your client calls it the "Thing" and he has designed a logo. Inside the case are various hardware components and software which is stored on semiconductor chips. The device plays music when a certain sequence of buttons has been pressed. Your client has prepared instructions for prospective customers.

- In such a case you might consider applicability of:

    ° copyright law for the computer programs;

    ° copyright law for the circuit layouts for the hardware components;

    ° copyright law for the instructions;

    ° copyright and trade-mark law for the logo;

    ° copyright law for the music as a musical work;

    ° industrial design law for the shape or appearance of the case;

    ° trade-mark law for the product name;

    ° trade-mark law for the product shape should it become distinctive over time;

    ° integrated circuit topography law for any custom-designed semiconductor chips;

    ° patent law for the combination of elements of the device;

    ° patent law for any process practised by the device or software;

    ° trade secret law for the concept and design details;

    ° trade secret law for any business plan, marketing plan or similar information; and

    ° moral rights claims on any copyright subject-matter.

(b) Example Two

- Your client comes to your office and describes for you a method or technique she has created. It is a method to make gold out of base metals. The method involves six steps. Your client calls the method the "Midas Touch" and he or she has designed a logo and has prepared instructions for prospective customers.

- In such a case you might consider applicability of:

  ° copyright law for the instructions;

  ° copyright and trade-mark law for the logo;

  ° trade-mark law for the name of the process;

  ° patent law for the process;

  ° patent law for a device (if any) used to practise the process;

  ° trade secret law for the concept and design details;

  ° trade secret law for any business plan, marketing plan or similar information; and

  ° moral rights claims on any copyright subject-matter.

2

CLIENT EDUCATION

2.1 INTRODUCTION

The purpose of this chapter is to provide an introduction to some basic legal issues surrounding Canadian patent law which may be of interest to the client.

Note that the information provided describes general rules in operation as at May 1999 and may be affected by the client's particular facts, subsequent law reform or judicial decisions. More detailed information may be found in certain sources identified in Appendix N.

- Except where indicated, this book is directed at patent law in Canada. Review the applicable law in other countries where protection is sought.

2.2 WHAT IS A PATENT?

- A patent is a statutory monopoly right with regard to a specific invention. *(For more detail on what constitutes an invention, see section 2.3, below)*.

- A patent provides the owner with the exclusive right to use the specific invention, to manufacture or have others manufacture that specific invention and to sell a product incorporating the specific invention.

- In each case, the scope of the exclusive right is determined by the claims of the patent.

- The statutory monopoly is for a specific period of time. *(In Canada that period is 20 years from the date of the application). Once that time has ended the exclusive rights are also ended. (See section 2.8, below.)*

- The inventor or owner (if not the inventor) has no rights unless a patent issues. Nor does the inventor or owner have
  any rights in a country unless a patent has been applied for
  and does issue from the applicable patent office in that
  country.

- In patent law, reference is made to "inventors" and "inventions" as contrasted with copyright law, where reference is to
  "authors" and "works."

- Examples of inventions are products and processes. Some
  well-known inventions include:

  ° the Thermos® brand vacuum bottle construction

  ° the machine to make Shredded Wheat brand cereal

  ° the incandescent light bulb and how it works

  ° a process for making Rice Krispies® brand cereal

  ° the chemical known by the trade-mark Lexan®

  ° the original telephone construction of Alexander Graham
    Bell

  ° the Windsurfer® brand sail board construction.

  *Note, in the foregoing examples, how trade-mark protection
  for the brand name of the product made using or related to the
  invention has been used to capture the goodwill related to the
  invention. Note as well that trade-mark rights can continue
  past the expiry of the patent rights. (See Chapter 1 for more information on trade-marks.)*

2.3 WHAT IS AN INVENTION?

- An invention is defined as any new and useful art, process,
  machine, manufacture or composition of matter, or any new
  and useful improvement in any art, process, machine, manufacture or composition of matter (section 2, *Patent Act*).

- An invention must be new and useful and may relate to:

  ° a product (*i.e.*, a novel combination of elements);

  ° a process (*i.e.*, a novel, logically interconnected series of steps to do something, such as a method or way to make a chemical, an algorithm, or a way to use a device);

  ° an apparatus (*i.e.*, a novel machine which can be used to make products or practice a process); or

  ° a composition of matter (*i.e.*, a combination of elements which result in a novel substance).

- An invention must have inventive merit or be non-obvious to a person skilled in the art (*see section 2.6.4, below*).

- If the invention is an improvement over something that existed before (such as a process, machine, product or composition of matter) the rights of the patentee do not extend to the prior thing (*i.e.*, the prior process, machine, product or composition of matter). In such case the patentee may be infringing on the rights of third parties in the prior thing (section 32, *Patent Act*). For example, if your client patented an improvement to a machine, then:

  ° your client may own rights to the improvement patent;

  ° your client would *not* have a right to use, manufacture or sell the machine (if the machine design itself was protected by patent) without the consent of the patentee of the machine patent (unless the prior patent has expired); and

  ° the patentee of the machine patent would *not* have a right to use, manufacture or sell the improvement claimed by your client's patent.

In such cases and depending on the specific situation there may be business merit in one or both of the parties selling or licensing rights to the other or otherwise cooperating.

- Examples of things which are *not* patentable inventions might include:

  ° a discovery of a new element or substance;

  ° works of authorship;

  ° mere scientific principles (section 27(8), *Patent Act*);

  ° abstract theorem (section 27(8), *Patent Act*);

  ° a mathematical method;

  ° mere information;

  ° speculations (*i.e.*, things not defined with precision or beyond reasonable prediction);

  ° computer programs, *per se* (see 12.02.01(g), *Manual of Patent Office Practice*) [*but an inventive process practiced by a programmed computer may be patentable*];

  ° aggregations (*i.e.*, things where the elements do not work together, such as a pencil and eraser, a nut cracker and dish, a cigarette lighter and ash tray, *etc.*);

  ° a scheme or method of playing a game or doing business (see 12.02.01(e), *Manual of Patent Office Practice*);

  ° a method of accounting or providing statistics on IQ tests;

  ° things which do not solve practical problems;

  ° things which serve no useful purpose;

  ° things which are not new or which are obvious;

  ° a method of medical treatment;

  ° a mental act such as an approach to thinking; or

° an invention with an illicit or immoral purpose.

- Patent law does *not* provide protection for:

    ° colours (*i.e.*, in the absence of any other feature) [*in such cases review applicability of trade-mark protection*];

    ° features, parts or components of an article which are solely visually appreciated [*in such cases review applicability of industrial design or copyright protection*];

    ° things which have no industrial utility [*in such cases review applicability of copyright or industrial design protection*]; or

    ° information, concepts or ideas [*in such cases review applicability of trade secret protection*].

2.4 NATURE OF THE RIGHTS

- Patent protection only arises on issue or grant (*i.e.*, registration) of the application for a patent.

- A patentee has rights only in countries where he or she has filed and obtained patent protection.

- A patent protects only the physical embodiment of the inventive idea or concept, not the idea or concept itself.

- The patentee's rights expire at the end of the term of the patent (or earlier if maintenance fees are not paid).

- There are no rights which are enforceable while a patent is pending. *Note however that a patentee can claim reasonable compensation for use of an invention after the patent application was laid open to the public but only if the patent actually issues.* (See section 55(2), *Patent Act.*)

- Unlike copyright, which only protects against copying (and certain other acts), an issued patent provides an exclusive monopoly to make, use or sell any product or process incorporating the claimed invention in the jurisdiction. (See section 42, *Patent Act.*) *That right may even be exercised against a person who independently invented a similar invention (but failed to make application for a patent before your client).*

- The rights in a granted patent are separate and apart from the rights in the product which practises or incorporates the invention. *For example the purchase of a patented product does not give the purchaser any rights to the patent.*

2.5 SCOPE OF PROTECTION

2.5.1 GENERAL

- Unless the invention is claimed in a valid, unexpired issued patent there are no rights under patent law.

- An unexpired issued patent provides the owner the exclusive right in Canada to make, use, construct and sell the invention claimed in the patent or authorize others to carry out such acts. (See section 42, *Patent Act.*)

2.5.2 RIGHTS UNDER A PATENT

(a) Use

- The right to use involves the right to practise the advantages offered by the patented product or process. *For example, the right to use an inventive brake system in your car or the right to use an inventive process to make widgets are illustrations of the exercise of the right to use. The patentee can authorize others to exercise these rights or any of them.*

- The right to use is implied on a sale authorized by the patentee. *For example, if the claim describes a certain machine, on the sale of that machine by the patentee (or with his or her authority) the purchaser may freely use the machine for the purpose for which it was intended.*

- Unless there is an agreement to the contrary, the patentee can no longer control the use of the machine in the market-place. The purchaser or a successor in title of the purchaser can freely use the machine without restriction from the patentee.

(b) Manufacture

- The right to manufacture involves the right to make or have made by others the patented product and in some cases to repair the patented products. The patentee can authorize others to exercise these rights.

- The right to make or authorize someone to make the invention is not exhausted after a sale authorized by the patentee. *For example, if the claim describes a certain product, after the manufacture and sale of the product by the patentee (or with his or her authority) the patentee may still control the manufacture of other copies of the product and in some cases repair of the specific product.*

- The purchaser of the product cannot manufacture additional copies of the product without consent of the patentee.

(c) Sell

- The right to sell involves the right to sell or have others sell the patented product or process. The patentee can authorize others to exercise these rights.

- The right to sell is exhausted after the first sale authorized by the patentee. *For example, if the claim describes a certain machine, after the sale of the machine by the patentee (or with his or her authority) the patentee can no longer control the subsequent sale of the machine in the marketplace.*

- The purchaser of the machine can freely resell the machine without restriction from the patentee.

2.6 FORMAL REQUIREMENTS FOR PATENT PROTECTION

- Certain formal conditions must be satisfied in order to come within the protection of the *Patent Act*:

  ° The invention must be protectable subject-matter.

  ° The invention must be new.

  ° The invention must be useful.

  ° The invention must show sufficient inventive merit.

- *Note that the inventor may be a resident of Canada or of a foreign country.*

2.6.1 SUBJECT-MATTER

- To be patentable, your client's technology must not only be an invention but it must be appropriate subject-matter for patent protection.

- For reasons of public policy, certain inventions may not be patentable. For example:

  ° A method of medical treatment may not be patentable: see *Tennessee Eastman Co. v. Canada (Commissioner of Patents)* (1972), [1974] S.C.R. 111, 8 C.P.R. (2d) 202 (S.C.C.) (a surgical method of bonding tissues).

  ° A computer program, *per se*, is not patentable: see *Schlumberger Ltd. v. Canada (Patent Commissioner)* (1981), 56 C.P.R. (2d) 204 (Fed. C.A.), leave to appeal to S.C.C. refused (1981), 63 C.P.R. (2d) 261n (S.C.C.) (a computer program).

  ° Certain living things may not be patentable if the disclosure requirements are not met: see *Pioneer Hi-Bred Ltd. v.*

Canada (Commissioner of Patents) (1989), 25 C.I.P.R. 1 (S.C.C.) (a new soya bean variety created by selective cross breeding).

° Multicellular living organisms: see *Harvard College v. Canada (Commissioner of Patents)* (1998), 79 C.P.R. (3d) 98 (Fed. T.D.) (a variety of transgenic mouse involving a claim to a mouse containing a foreign genetic sequence).

° *See the list in section 2.3, above.*

• A valuable part of a technology may often lie in the business or other information related to the invention or its use. This information might *not* be protected by a patent. Depending on the circumstances the information might be protected under trade secret law by imposing obligations of confidence on users of the information. (*See Chapter 1 for more details.*)

• The goodwill and reputation relating to an invention may be protected through use of trade-mark rights. (*See Chapter 1 for more details.*)

• The physical appearance of products might be protectable, in applicable circumstances, by copyright or industrial design registration. (*See Chapter 1 for more details.*)

2.6.2 UTILITY

• Patent law is only intended to protect inventions which serve some useful purpose. Utility is a question of fact.

• The technology must solve some practical problem, thus speculative technologies are not patentable.

• The technology must work, it must do what the inventor claims it can do. *If it does not work it is not useful.* See *TRW Inc. v. Walbar of Canada Inc.* (1991), 39 C.P.R. (3d) 176 (Fed. C.A.), leave to appeal to S.C.C. refused (1992), 42 C.P.R. (3d) v (note) (S.C.C.).

- There should be no breach of a fundamental law of science. *For example, a perpetual motion machine is in violation of the 2nd law of thermodynamics. In such cases it is unlikely that the proposed technology actually works.*

2.6.3 NOVELTY

- An invention must satisfy a requirement of novelty in order to be capable of being granted patent protection; it must be the first in the world; it must be new.

- Review the client's prior use or disclosure of the invention and determine if the activity made the invention available to the public.

- *Failure to address issues of novelty and disclosure may result in loss of rights!*

- *See section 3.1.1, below, for further and more detailed discussion of novelty.*

2.6.4 INVENTIVE MERIT

- To be an invention a technology must not be obvious to a person skilled in the art. (See *Diversified Products Corp. v. Tye-Sil Corp.* (1991), 35 C.P.R. (3d) 350 (Fed. C.A.), and section 28.3, *Patent Act.*)

- The applicable art is that related to the invention. *For example, if the invention is a device in the oil and gas industry then the applicable art should be in that industry or any directly related industry.*

- In the United States, the notional person skilled in the art is an ordinary skilled person.

- In Canada, the notional person skilled in the art is an unimaginative skilled technician. (See *Beloit Canada Ltée./Ltd. v. Valmet Oy* (1986), 8 C.P.R. (3d) 289 (Fed. C.A.), leave to appeal to S.C.C. refused (1986), 8 C.I.P.R. xlvii (note) (S.C.C.).)

- The test for obviousness is:

  ° In light of the prior art of which the person skilled in the art would be aware at the time the invention was made and with his or her general knowledge and information and literature available to him or her at the time, would the unimaginative skilled technician have come directly and without difficulty to the invention?

- For examples, see *Beecham Canada Ltd. v. Procter & Gamble Co.* (1982), 61 C.P.R. (2d) 1 (Fed. C.A.); *Baxter Travenol Laboratories of Canada Ltd. v. Cutter (Canada) Ltd.* (1983), 68 C.P.R. (2d) 179 (Fed. C.A.), leave to appeal refused (1983), 72 C.P.R. (2d) 287, 51 N.R. 238 (S.C.C.) (a blood bag collection system); *Windsurfing International Inc. v. Trilantic Corp.* (1985), 8 C.P.R. (3d) 241 (Fed. C.A.), additional reasons at (1986), 8 C.P.R. (3d) 270 (Fed. C.A.) (a sail board); *Reading & Bates Construction Co. v. Baker Energy Resources Corp.* (1987), 18 C.P.R. (3d) 180 (Fed. C.A.) (a liner invention and a pull-back invention used in a pre-bored path with a view to installing a pipeline).

- This is a difficult test to apply. You must ascertain:

  ° What is the relevant art?

  ° Who is the notional unimaginative skilled technician?

  ° What is the level of knowledge of the notional unimaginative skilled technician?

  ° What information and general knowledge would be available to such a person in the relevant art?

- One should not rely on hindsight analysis. See *Reading & Bates Construction Co. v. Baker Energy Resources Corp.* (1987), 18 C.P.R. (3d) 180 (Fed. C.A.) in which the following example of the expression that one is "wiser after the fact" are noted, including: "Nothing is easier to say, after the event, that the thing was obvious and involved no invention" (*Non-Drip Measure Co. v. Stranger's Ltd.* (1943), 60 R.P.C. 135 (U.K. H.L.) at p. 142).

- Since inventions often appear obvious once you know what the invention is, you often look to certain objective indications which suggest the invention was not obvious before the application was filed. The test applied by the court is an objective test: *Reading & Bates Construction Co. v. Baker Energy Resources Corp.* (1987), 18 C.P.R. (3d) 180 (Fed. C.A.).

- Some objective indications are:

  ° other persons did not assess likelihood of success of the unmade invention so as to warrant a test or trial of the technology;

  ° prior work in the field points to a different solution (*examples might be found in published articles, trade journals, etc.*);

  ° the industry (art) thought it would not work (*examples might be found in published articles, trade journals, etc.*);

  ° the invention meets an unfulfilled need in the marketplace (*if the need existed a reasonable period of time before the application was filed and if the invention was obvious, someone would have made the invention before; since no one did make the invention before then it must have been non-obvious*);

  ° substantial commercial success of the invention (*substantial commercial success is an indication that there may be an unfulfilled need in the marketplace which has been addressed by the invention, as noted above*); or

  ° substantial infringement of the invention (*substantial infringement is an indication that there may be an unfulfilled need in the marketplace which has been addressed by the invention and which the inventor has not been able to fulfil himself or herself resulting in the infringing activity by the pirates).*

- *It has been suggested that an invention will provoke a reaction akin to "Aha!" or "Why did I not think of that?"*

- *If the invention is a substantial advance in the art, why was it not done before?*

2.7 OWNERSHIP

2.7.1 GENERAL RULE

- The basic principle is that the inventor is the owner of the invention. Note that only the inventor or his or her legal representative may apply for a patent in respect of the invention. (see section 27(1), *Patent Act*). The question of *who is the inventor is a question of fact.*

- The identity of the inventor is tested against the claims in the patent: *Ernest Scragg & Sons Ltd. v. Leesona Corp.* (1964), 45 C.P.R. 1 (Can. Ex. Ct.).

- Merely advancing an idea or suggestion in terms of an objective or an end result is not, by itself, inventorship: *Comstock Canada v. Electec Ltd.* (1991), 38 C.P.R. (3d) 29 (Fed. T.D.).

- The date of invention is that date when the inventor can prove he or she first formulated, either in writing or orally, a description which affords the means for making that which is invented: *Rice v. Christiani & Nielsen*, [1930] 4 D.L.R. 401 (S.C.C.), affirmed [1931] 4 D.L.R. 273 (Canada P.C.); or for a process when it is first used: *Ernest Scragg & Sons Ltd. v. Leesona Corp.* (1964), 45 C.P.R. 1 (Can. Ex. Ct.); *Comstock Canada v. Electec Ltd.* (1991), 38 C.P.R. (3d) 29 (Fed. T.D.).

- The invention must originate in the inventor's mind, not be borrowed from elsewhere: *Gerrard Wire Tying Machines Co.*

v. Cary Manufacturing Co., [1926] 3 D.L.R. 374 (Can. Ex. Ct.); *Comstock Canada v. Electec Ltd.* (1991), 38 C.P.R. (3d) 29 (Fed. T.D.).

- A misnomer of the inventor does not, *per se*, affect the validity of a patent especially where the patentee holds all rights of all inventors: *Dec International Inc. v. A.L. LaCombe & Associates Ltd.* (1989), 26 C.P.R. (3d) 193 (Fed. T.D.); *Procter & Gamble Co. v. Bristol-Myers Canada Ltd.* (1978), 39 C.P.R. (2d) 145 (Fed. T.D.), affirmed (1979), 42 C.P.R. (2d) 33 (Fed. C.A.), leave to appeal refused (1979), 42 C.P.R. (2d) 33n (S.C.C.).

2.7.2 HIRED TO INVENT

- The general rule is that if a servant, while in the employ of his or her master, makes an invention, that invention belongs to the servant and not the master: *Bloxam v. Elsee* (1827), 108 E.R. 415 (Eng. K.B.); *W.J. Gage Ltd. v. Sugden*, [1967] 2 O.R. 151 (Ont. H.C.); *Comstock Canada Ltd. v. Electec Ltd.* (1991), 38 C.P.R. (3d) 29 (Fed. T.D.).

- There are two lines of cases dealing with situations where an employee is hired to make inventions:

  ° The older cases hold that it is an implied term in a contract of employment that an employee is a trustee for his or her employer of any invention made in the course of employment unless there is an agreement to the contrary: *Sterling Engineering Co. v. Patchett* (1955), 72 R.P.C. 50 (U.K. H.L.), approved and adopted in *W.J. Gage Ltd. v. Sugden*, [1967] 2 O.R. 151 (Ont. H.C.).

  ° Some newer cases look more specifically at the scope of the employment and if the employee's work is not to make inventions or advance technology then the employee owns the invention: *Comstock Canada Ltd. v. Electec Ltd.* (1991), 38 C.P.R. (3d) 29 (Fed. T.D.).

- Currently, and absent any agreement on the point, an employee will own an invention made by him or her unless:

  ° there is an agreement to the contrary;

  ° the person was employed for the express purpose of inventing or innovating; or

  ° the person is under a fiduciary or similar obligation to the employer.

- Factors considered by the court include:

  ° whether the employee was hired for the express purpose of inventing;

  ° whether the employee, at the time of hire, had previously made inventions;

  ° whether an employer had incentive plans encouraging product development;

  ° whether the conduct of the employee once the invention was created suggested ownership by the employer;

  ° whether the invention is the product of the problem the employee was instructed to solve, *i.e.*, was it his or her duty to make inventions;

  ° whether the employee's invention arose following his or her consultation through normal company channels (*i.e.*, was help sought);

  ° whether the employee was dealing with highly confidential information or confidential work; and

  ° whether it was a term of the employee's employment that he or she could not use the ideas which he or she developed to his or her own advantage.

(See *Comstock Canada Ltd. v. Electec Ltd.* (1991), 38 C.P.R. (3d) 29 (Fed. T.D.).)

- Review these factors as well as those identified in Chapter 1 with the client.

- *Note that the copyright and industrial design ownership rules are different. This may result in different owners of copyright, industrial design and patent rights in the same invention/work/design.*

- The *Patent Act* provides special rules for inventions made by officers, servants or employees of the Crown or of a corporation that is an agent or servant of the Crown. In such cases if the person makes the invention within the scope of his or her duties and employment related to munitions of war, all benefits of the invention and any patent which issues in relation to the invention are assigned to the Minister of National Defence (see section 20, *Patent Act*). Inventions made by Crown employees are governed by the *Public Servants Inventions Act* (Canada). These rules can make it very difficult for a business to collaborate on research and development projects with federal Crown departments, agencies or corporations.

2.7.3 FIDUCIARIES

- An inventor may be obligated to assign his or her invention to a person (typically an employer) with whom the inventor has a fiduciary or similar relationship: *Comstock Canada Ltd. v. Electec Ltd.* (1991), 38 C.P.R. (3d) 29 (Fed. T.D.).

- Care must be exercised to determine if the inventor is in such a relationship of high trust. The mere fact that an inventor held a senior position in a company does not deprive the inventor of an invention if that is not what he or she was hired to do: *Anemostat (Scotland) Ltd. v. Michaelis*, [1957] R.P.C. 167 (U.K.).

- A manager's position is radically different from that of a tradesperson. The manager has a fundamental or fiduciary duty to extend all of his or her effort, skill, knowledge and inventive powers, in what ever way possible, to promote the efficiency and success of the employer and does not need to be specifically directed or encouraged to do so: see *Worthington Pumping Engine Co. v. Moore* (1902), 20 R.P.C. 41 (Eng. Ch. Div.); *Edisonia Ltd. v. Forse* (1908), 25 R.P.C. 546 (Eng. Ch. Div.); *Canadian Aero Service Ltd. v. O'Malley* (1973), 11 C.P.R. (2d) 206 (S.C.C.), cited as authority for this proposition in *Comstock Canada Ltd. v. Electec Ltd.* (1991), 38 C.P.R. (3d) 29 (Fed. T.D.).

- A director or senior officer is precluded from obtaining for himself or herself, either secretly or without the approval of the company, any property or business advantage belonging to the company or for which it has been negotiating: *Canadian Aero Service Ltd. v. O'Malley* (1973), 11 C.P.R. (2d) 206 (S.C.C.).

- An employee cannot disclose confidential information of the employer: *Scapa Dryers (Can.) Ltd. v. Fardeau* (1971), 1 C.P.R. (2d) 199 (Que. S.C.).

2.7.4 SHOP RIGHT

- The U.S. cases have developed the concept of a "shop right". This is a non-exclusive right of an employer to use an invention made by and owned by an employee where the invention was made with the employer's tools or resources.

- This concept has not been well received in Canadian law: see *W.J. Gage Ltd. v. Sugden*, [1967] 2 O.R. 151 (Ont. H.C.).

- There are several older cases which have appeared to find implied rights of an employer to use an employee's invention: see *Imperial Supply Co. v. Grand Trunk Railway* (1912), 14 Ex. C.R. 88 (Can. Ex. Ct.); *Willard's Chocolates Ltd. v. Bardsley* (1928), 35 O.W.N. 92 (Ont. H.C.).

2.7.5 CONTRACTS TO THE CONTRARY

- If the parties enter into a written agreement specifically and expressly addressing the ownership of the rights in the invention, the courts will give force to that agreement.

- If the terms of employment are not expressly clear, consider the factors discussed in section 2.7.2, above, and whether or not a fiduciary or similar relationship of trust exists.

2.8 TERM

- A patent based on an application filed on or after October 1, 1989 is granted for 20 years from the date of application (section 44, *Patent Act*).

- A patent based on an application filed before October 1, 1989 is granted for 17 years from the date of issue of the patent (section 45, *Patent Act*).

- The term of patents based on applications filed on or after October 1, 1989 may be limited if maintenance fees are not paid within the time provided (sections 6.3 and 46(2), *Patent Act*).

- Once the term expires, the rights of the patentee end and the invention may be used, manufactured and sold by any person.

- *Watch carefully whether or not improvement patents have been issued after the base patent has expired.*

- Exercise care to avoid infringement of improvements claimed in valid unexpired patents.

2.9 NOTICE

- The placement of a notice is not required under Canadian law, however, it might be argued that placing an accurate notice provides notice of the patentee's rights which may facilitate the patentee's ability to claim punitive damages in an appropriate case.

- The statement "patent pending" or "patent applied for" may be applied to articles after the patent application has been filed, although these notices have no legal effect in Canada.

- It may be an offence under the patent laws of several countries (such as the United States and United Kingdom) to place a notice falsely claiming to have filed a patent application. While no such prohibition exists for Canada, caution is suggested due to the provisions of section 75 of the *Patent Act* which provides for certain offences where one:

  - without the consent of the patentee places the patentee's name or an imitation thereof on anything made by the person; or

  - without the consent of the patentee marks "patented", "letters patent", "Queen's (or King's) Patent", or "patented" on anything with an intent to imitate any mark of the patentee or of deceiving the public that the thing was produced with the consent of the patentee.

2.10 FILING

2.10.1 NORMAL APPLICATIONS

- The patent application must be forwarded to the Patent Office within one year of the invention being made public in Canada. (See sections 2.6.3, above, and 3.1, below, and section 27(1), *Patent Act* for more details.)

- Reliance on the one-year grace period may result in loss of rights in other countries. (*See section 3.1.2, below.*)

- *Failure to make application for a patent within one year of any publication or making available to the public may result in loss of rights.*

- The address and telephone number of the Patent Office is:

  Commissioner of Patents

Industry Canada
50 Victoria Street
Place du Portage, Phase I
Hull, Quebec
K1A 0C9
Telephone: (819) 997-1936.

• Further details of the application process are described in Chapters 4 and 5.

2.10.2 PROVISIONAL PATENT APPLICATIONS

• Both Canada and the United States permit the filing of an application with relaxed filing requirements. Such patent applications are commonly known as provisional patent applications. A provisional patent application is typically based on the disclosure provided by the inventor and may not have claims.

• Some inventors appear to believe that a provisional patent application provides an inexpensive informal way to obtain substantive patent rights. Caution must be exercised in filing a provisional patent application. Patent rights may be lost if proper attention is not provided in the preparation of a provisional patent application.

• Some specific cautions regarding filing a provisional patent application include:

   ° Merely because the filing requirements are relaxed does not mean the inventor is relieved of the obligation to provide an enabling disclosure or, as applicable, disclose best mode or satisfy other substantive patent law filing requirements. Inattention to these issues may impair the ability to enforce such rights as they arise.

   ° Since the subsequent patent will be based on the disclosure provided in the provisional application, insufficient care or attention to the scope and detail of the draft provisional patent application may limit rights. Since the scope of any subsequent patent will be based on the provisional patent application, the failure to fully disclose the invention or properly flesh out the features of the invention may result in loss of rights in the event a subsequent patent application filed by a third party claims the applicable subject matter.

° Specifically, the inventor should not expect that he or she can merely file a soon-to-be published paper as a provisional patent application and expect to obtain extensive or, perhaps, any patent rights. Significant value is often added to a patent application as a result of a proper interaction between the inventor and patent agent during the drafting process. This process typically expands the scope of the invention and provides for less opportunities to design around any resulting patent.

° If the inventor is filing a provisional patent application to seek to provide a filing basis prior to presenting the invention at a conference or symposium there is a danger that the oral presentation or answers to questions may disclose material inventive subject matter which was not included in the provisional application. If that is the case then the novelty rules would prohibit patent protection for such disclosed elements in absolute novelty countries and the time will have begun to run for filing purposes in partial novelty countries.

° Concern has been expressed that a provisional patent application without any claims may not be a basis for a convention filing in some countries. See section 2.11 and 3.3 for more details on the use of convention filings. As a result, prudent practice suggests the patent agent should add at least one claim in any provisional patent application.

° There may be a concern if the more formal filing filed to supersede the provisional patent application may not have identical disclosure and that intervening rights may have arisen or some of the new matter introduced may be unpatentable. Because of the forgoing types of issues we can expect that patents originally filed as provisional patent applications may be subject to some greater scrutiny in litigation.

° If your client wishes to file a provisional patent application it is suggested that the inventor be advised of the risks which may be associated with this approach particularly if a very casual or informal approach to preparation of the disclosure is adopted by the client. If in doubt consult with a patent agent or patent lawyer.

2.11 INTERNATIONAL PRIORITY

By virtue of the Convention for the Protection of Industrial Property made in Paris ("Paris Convention") and subsequently amended, an applicant for patent protection may file a corresponding application in the appropriate government office of other member countries and claim the priority of the first filing date but only if such subsequent filings are made within one year of the first filing date. (See section 3.3.1, below, and Appendix I for details on the Convention; use of Convention priority is described in section 3.3, below.)

Canada also adheres to the Patent Cooperation Treaty ("PCT") which provides a similar method of managing foreign filings. (See section 3.3.2, below, and Appendix J for details on the Treaty.)

- *Canadian applicants making their first filing for an invention must be aware that foreign applications filed up to one year before the Canadian application is filed may have priority to obtain the grant of a patent for the invention.*

- *Always review the present status of any signatory to an international treaty prior to reliance on the treaty provisions.*

- Many Canadian inventors file their first (or simultaneously file a) patent application in the United States Patent and Trademark Office. Some of the reasons to do so include:

  ° If the inventor plans to negotiate licence or similar agreements with U.S.-based companies regarding the commercial exploitation of the invention, such companies tend to see U.S. filings as more significant than only a Canadian application.

  ° The cost to file in the U.S. is often roughly the same as the cost to file in Canada.

° The U.S. Patent and Trademark Office is very efficient. The first office action may be received often within eight to fifteen months of filing. This often gives the inventor the benefit of a substantial review of the merits of the patent application before the inventor must decide whether or not to commit substantial funds to foreign applications. This, in turn, tends to give the inventor a better basis for that business decision. *Note that the longer delay period under the PCT process and the search reports available under that process may also be of similar assistance to the client.*

° The U.S. does not give complete convention rights under the Paris Convention. As a result, applicants often wish to file early in the U.S. to preserve their rights.

° In the United States, the first to invent wins in a contest between two applicants. Until December 8, 1993, only inventive activity in the U.S. by a foreign applicant qualified to create an invention date for U.S. purposes (see 35 U.S.C. s. 104 of the U.S. patent law). This created an important legal reason to file first in the U.S. since the filing of the application often created the earliest invention date for the Canadian inventor.

° The U.S. rule, looking only to U.S. activity to create a U.S. invention, arguably acts as a non-tariff barrier to trade and substantially favours U.S. residents over foreign inventors. Under the *North American Free Trade Agreement* ("NAFTA"), the United States did not abandon this discriminatory rule. The U.S. did, however, extend the regions in which conduct may establish a U.S. invention date to Canada and Mexico and any subsequent NAFTA country. The U.S. *NAFTA Implementation Act* amended 35 U.S.C. s. 104 to permit patent applicants or patent owners to prove an invention date by reference to activities and knowledge or use of the invention in Canada, Mexico, the United States or any future NAFTA country. As a result, Canadian inventors may now benefit from the advantages of this discriminatory rule *vis-à-vis* non-NAFTA (*i.e.*, Asian or European) inventors. *With the NAFTA changes, this particular reason to file first in the U.S. no longer appears to exist.*

° The patent application is kept strictly confidential until or unless the application is issued. As a result (and if no foreign or Canadian applications are filed which would be laid open to the public 18 months after the application date in most countries), the application can be kept completely confidential until issue. This means that the inventor is able to avoid disclosure of the details of the invention until issue and the risk of such disclosure if the invention did not issue.

• It is strongly recommended that you use a registered U.S. patent agent to file in the United States Patent Office. *Many Canadian patent agents are also registered U.S. patent agents.*

• Given the similarities between the Canadian and U.S. patent systems and the requirements of very similar information, the applicant may be able to achieve some cost savings by filing both Canadian and U.S. applications. You should discuss these issues with the patent agent.

2.12 EXEMPTIONS

• The *Patent Act* prohibits the use, manufacture or sale of patented inventions without the permission of the owner of the patent, however, certain limited exemptions exist permitting conduct to be carried out which would otherwise infringe rights under a valid unexpired patent.

2.12.1 WHAT YOUR CLIENT MAY USE

• Your client may use:

° inventions where the patent rights have been dedicated to the public;

° inventions where the patentee has given permission for the use;

° inventions where the term of the patent has expired [for most cases 20 years from the date of application (section 44, *Patent Act*) or for patents based on applications filed before October 1, 1989, 17 years from the date of application (section 45, *Patent Act*)];

° inventions where the maintenance fees have not been paid within the applicable time and therefore the term of the patent expired early (section 46(2), *Patent Act*); or

° inventions made and protected in other countries but not filed and issued in Canada; or

° under an exemption under the *Patent Act*; or

° if the client is the Government of Canada, in certain circumstances the Government may use any patented invention and must pay the patentee the amount the Commissioner of Patents determines is reasonable compensation for the use (see sections 19 and 19.1, *Patent Act*).

2.12.2 EXCEPTIONS

• Section 23 of the *Patent Act* provides that a patent will not extend to prevent use of any invention in any ship, vessel, aircraft or land vehicle of any country which enters Canada temporarily or accidentally. This provision applies so long as the invention is used solely for the needs of the ship, vessel, aircraft or land vehicle and is not used to manufacture goods to be sold in Canada or to be exported from Canada.

• It is not an infringement of a patent to make, use or sell the patented invention solely for purposes specified in section 55.2(1) of the Act to make, construct or use the invention, during any period provided by regulation, for the manufacture and storage of articles intended for sale after the term of the patent expires (section 55.2(2), *Patent Act*).

- It is not an infringement of a patent to make, use or sell the patented invention solely for purposes reasonably related to the development or submission of information required under any law in Canada, or of a province, that regulates the manufacture, construction, use or sale of a product (section 55.2(1), *Patent Act*).

- Section 56(1) of the *Patent Act* provides that a person who, before the claim date in a patent, purchases, acquires or constructs the invention in respect of which, subsequently, the patent issues has the right without liability to the patentee to continue to use and sell to others the specific article, machine, manufacture or composition of matter patented and which was purchased, constructed or acquired. See *Merck & Co. v. Apotek Inc.*, [1995] 2 F.C. 723 (Fed. C.A.), leave to appeal refused (1995), 63 C.P.R. (3d) v (S.C.C.) for a review of the operation of section 56.

2.12.3 OBTAINING PERMISSION TO USE

- The need for permission (and risks of infringement) may be identified as a result of doing applicable searches. (See section 4.1 on searches, below.)

- Generally, a formal negotiation is involved to obtain permission from a patentee to use the rights under the patent.

- The permission should be recorded in writing specifying the scope of the permission, the rights which may be used and all other relevant terms.

- If permission is sought informally, your client should record the permission with at least a confirming letter providing specifics of the terms of the permission and describing the rights under the invention which may be used. That informal licence should satisfy all the requirements to be an enforceable contract.

- The permission (licence) may be recorded in the Patent Office *(see section 6.1.1, below). Such recordation is strongly encouraged to provide rights against third parties.*

- In certain exceptional cases, a licensor's refusal to license on reasonable commercial terms may provide a basis for seeking a compulsory licence under the provisions of section 65 of the *Patent Act.*

2.13 ADVANTAGES OF PATENT PROTECTION

- Patent protection has several advantages over copyright or industrial design protection:

  ° An issued patent may provide the exclusive right in Canada to use, manufacture and sell the invention. *These are substantial monopoly rights.*

  ° The right arising from an issued patent may even be exercised against a person who independently invented a similar invention (but failed to file before your client). *Independent creation, if proven, is a defence to a copyright infringement action.*

  ° Copyright protects only the form of expression of an idea and not the idea itself. Where there are many possible forms of a work expressing a similar concept or set of ideas, such as in a number of cookbooks, paintings of similar scenes, it is apparent that the copyright provides somewhat limited protection and not over the underlying concepts or theme.

  ° Copyright and industrial design do not protect useful features of a work or design.

- There are a large number of exemptions which are available to permit copying or use of a work in unique circumstances. There are few and very limited exemptions under patent law.

2.14 DISADVANTAGES OF PATENT PROTECTION

- When contrasted with copyright protection, patent protection has a number of disadvantages:

° Patent rights only arise on registration. As a result, any defect in the application or failure to apply in time may result in loss of rights. There is no cost or formality involved in the creation of enforceable copyright.

° Patent protection is only available for inventions which are new. Copyright, on the other hand, provides protection for any original work whether or not it is new.

° Patent rights are available for a term of 20 years from the date of application (or for patent applications filed prior to October 1, 1989, for 17 years from date of issue). The maximum term of protection is 20 years. The term of protection of copyright is substantially longer. Copyright for most works exists for the term of the life of the author plus the end of the year in which the author dies plus 50 years.

° It may take several years to obtain grant of a patent. This may be a serious disadvantage for industries where the marketplace changes very rapidly. By contrast, copyright arises automatically on creation of an original work. *Note that the patent application process may be expedited in certain circumstances.*

° Since a patent is a public document, trade secret protection may not also be utilized to protect the invention so disclosed.

° The *Copyright Act* gives the copyright holder certain rights in members of certain international treaties without any filings or formalities in those counties. By contrast, patent protection is only available where patent applications are filed and patents actually issue from the respective patent office.

3

THINGS TO WATCH FOR

3.1 PRIOR PUBLICATION OR DISCLOSURE

- Prior publication or disclosure may affect the ability to obtain patent protection.

- *Note also that publication or disclosure may affect the extent of protection available for the technology under industrial design, trade secret and other law.*

3.1.1 NOVELTY

- An invention must satisfy a requirement of novelty in order to be capable of being granted patent protection.

- You should review the client's prior use or disclosure of the invention and determine if the activity made the invention available to the public. *(See section 1.4.6, above.)*

- *Failure to address issues of novelty and disclosure may result in loss of rights.*

(a) Requirements Generally

- To be protectable the invention must not only be new, it:

  ° must not be anticipated by another event or document which shows the same thing;

  ° must not be anticipated by another event or document which describes essentially the same thing for practical purposes; and

° must not have been available to the public (*see below for more details on this point*).

(b) Assessing Novelty

- To determine the novelty of the invention:

  ° examine each of the elements of the invention;

  ° look at the invention as a whole;

  ° identify the relevant prior art; and

  ° review the prior art in the context of what would be understood by a person skilled in the art (*see below for the level of skill expected of such a person*).

- For the purposes of assessing novelty, you must find the same thing or the same thing for practical purposes in one document. You may not make a mosaic of such documents. (*Note all such documents are also assessed from the perspective of inventive merit or non-obviousness. See section 2.6.4, above.*)

- For example, the application of a known method to known materials but where the method had never before been applied to such materials may constitute novelty: see *Canada (Commissioner of Patents) v. Ciba Ltd.*, [1959] S.C.R. 378 (S.C.C.).

(c) Tests for Prior Art

- For purposes of attacking novelty, the prior art must:

  ° give an exact prior description;

  ° give directions which will inevitably result in something in the claims;

  ° give clear and unmistakable directions to make the thing;

° give information which for purposes of practical utility is equal to that given by the subject patent;

° give information which enables a person struggling with the same problem to find an answer;

° give information to a person of ordinary knowledge such that he or she at once perceives the invention;

° teach an inevitable result which can only be proved by experiment;

(See *Johnson Controls Ltd. v. Varta Batteries Ltd.* (1984), 80 C.P.R. (2d) 1 (Fed. C.A.), leave to appeal refused (1984), 56 N.R. 398n (S.C.C.) (a battery case invention) and *Reeves Brothers Inc. v. Toronto Quilting & Embroidery Ltd.* (1978), 43 C.P.R. (2d) 145 (Fed. T.D.) and cases cited therein.)

• In order to show anticipation not all of the elements above are required though some are essential. See *Free World Trust c. Électro Santé Inc.* (1997), (sub nom. *Free World Trust v. Électro Santé Inc.*) 81 C.P.R. (3d) 456 (C.A. Qué.), leave to appeal allowed (1998), (sub nom, *Free World Trust v. Électro Santé Inc.*) 81 C.P.R. (3d) 456n (C.S.C.)

(d) Filing Requirement

(i) Patent Applications under Convention or Treaty Rights

• For foreign patent applications filed under convention or treaty rights:

° an application must have been filed by the client in the Canadian Patent Office before any application for a patent describing the same invention was filed in Canada by any other person before the claim date of the client's foreign application; or

   ° an application must have been filed by the client in the Canadian Patent Office before the claim date of an application for a patent describing the same invention of a convention or treaty application is filed in Canada by any other person at any time and where the claim date of that conflicting application precedes the claim date of the client's foreign application.

See sections 27(1), 28.1, and 28.2, *Patent Act*.)

- For example, to satisfy these requirements:

X	Y	Time
Your client's application is filed first elsewhere and the Canadian application for priority is first in time.	The competing application is filed later; and the claim date of any competing application is later	

(ii) Where no Convention or Treaty Rights Apply

- For all other patent applications filed in the Canadian Patent Office:

   ° the client's application must be filed before any application for a patent describing the same invention was filed in Canada by any other person; or

   ° the client's application must be filed before any application for a patent describing the same invention is filed as a convention or treaty application in Canada by any other person and the claim date of the conflicting application precedes the claim date of the client's application.

See section 27, 28.1, 28.2 *Patent Act*.)

- For example, to satisfy these requirements:

──────── X ──────── Y ──────────────────────────► Time

Your client's application   The competing
is filed first   application is filed later;
                                   and the claim date of
                                   any competing
                                   application is later

(e) Disclosure Rules

- In many countries no disclosure which results in the invention being made available to the public in that country or elsewhere (including in Canada) may be carried out before a valid patent application is filed in that country's patent office. Such countries are called "absolute novelty jurisdictions."

- In Canada and the U.S., there is a limited right to carry out certain disclosures before a patent application is filed in that country. *Reliance on this grace period may result in loss of rights in other countries.* Countries that permit some limited disclosure prior to filing are called "partial novelty jurisdictions".

- In Canada, except for the limited disclosures by the inventor or through the inventor *(see section 3.1.2, below)*, the invention must not have been disclosed by any person such that the invention became available to the public before the date of filing of the application or the claim date of the application (section 28.2(1)(b), *Patent Act*).

- The inventor may still seek protection in Canada if the inventor or a person who obtained knowledge of the invention from the inventor may disclose the invention such that it becomes available to the public in Canada or elsewhere but only if such disclosure occurred *in no more than one year before the filing of the application* (section 28.2(1)(a), *Patent Act*). *(See, however, section 3.1.2, below. Use of this grace period may result in loss of rights in other countries.)*

- The novelty rules in the United States are different. Generally to be able to make a valid patent application in the U.S. Patent and Trademark Office, the invention must:

° not have been made available to the public in the U.S. more than one year before the application is filed in the U.S. Patent and Trademark Office; and

° not have been described in a printed publication anywhere more than one year before the application is filed in the U.S. Patent and Trademark Office.

• Typically an inventor may seek to use convention priority to manage the filing of the patent application in foreign countries including managing foreign filings in relation to public disclosure of the invention subsequent to the first (priority) application. (*See section 3.3, below, for a detailed introduction to use of convention priority.*)

• Review the current status of any specific novelty requirements in each country in which you seek protection for your client's invention.

3.1.2 GRACE PERIOD

• In Canada, in order to make a valid patent application the application must have been filed no less than one year after the invention has been published or otherwise made available to the public in Canada or elsewhere.

• In the United States, in order to make a valid patent application the application must be filed no less than one year after:

° any disclosure of the invention was carried out in the United States; and

° the invention was published in a printed publication anywhere.

• *In summary:*

° To maximize the ability to make a valid patent application anywhere in the world no disclosure of the invention should be carried out anywhere before the application is filed in the applicable patent office(s). *(See section 3.3, below, on use of convention priority.)*

° To maximize the ability to make a valid patent application only in the United States and Canada no disclosure of the invention should be carried out anywhere and no description of the invention published in a printed publication anywhere in either case more than one year before the application is filed in the United States Patent and Trademark Office and the Canadian Patent Office.

° To maximize the ability to make a valid patent application in the United States only no disclosure of the invention should be carried out in the United States and no description of the invention published in a printed publication anywhere in either case more than one year before the application is filed in the United States Patent and Trademark Office.

• Caution should be exercised if it is desired to protect the invention in other countries.

• Reliance on a grace period will preclude the ability to file valid patent applications in many countries. Some countries may provide no grace period following a publication in which to file a valid application for patent protection.

3.2 THIRD-PARTY INTERESTS

• Ownership rights in an invention arise from making a contribution to the invention. *(See section 2.7, above.)*

• There may be third-party interests in an invention which was developed by several persons.

• The operation of the ownership rules may result in a third party having an ownership claim in critical parts of an invention.

- It is important to identify all true inventorship contributions to an invention and address any issues arising from ownership or other interests owned or claimed by third parties.

3.3 CONVENTION PRIORITY

- Use of convention priority may be an effective way to seek to establish protection for the technology in other countries. Canada is a member of two important international conventions: the Paris Convention ("Convention") and the Patent Cooperation Treaty ("PCT"). While the operation of these treaties has some similarities, there are some important differences:

  ° The Paris Convention is the easiest to use and incurs no additional cost or complexity on the filing of the application. Given that simplicity, the general use of a convention to manage international filings and a variety of the benefits arising therefrom are described for the Paris Convention in sections 3.3.1(a) to (d), below. Similar concepts may apply for use of the PCT.

  ° The PCT has some advantages over the Paris Convention but it is more complex and may result in incurring additional costs early in the filing process. (*The operation of the PCT is described in section 3.3.2 below.*)

3.3.1 PARIS CONVENTION

- Nationals of member countries may utilize the provisions of the Convention to facilitate their foreign filings in other member countries of the Convention.

- This Convention operates to permit an applicant to file an application for a patent in respect of an invention in one country and file corresponding applications in other member countries of the Convention so long as the corresponding applications are filed within 12 months of the first application.

- By relying on the Convention, the applicant has a priority date (the date of the first filing) and can claim that priority date in other member countries so long as the corresponding applications are filed within 12 months of the priority date. *In effect this allows the applicant to back-date his or her applications filed in the other countries as if they were filed on the priority date and thereby have an application with a priority date before any public disclosure activity. Of course if there was public disclosure activity before the first filing one must review the domestic law of each country in order to determine whether or not a valid application may still be filed.*

- The use of Convention priority works best if the first (priority) application is filed before any public activity with the invention anywhere. In all other cases you should review the possible loss of rights due to the public activity under the domestic law of the countries in which you wish to file.

- *Always review the domestic law of the country in which you seek to file.*

- *Always review the treaty status of the country in which you seek to file.*

- *Note that some countries are not members of a treaty or convention and the following approaches may not work in such countries.*

- *If in doubt, get help!*

(a) Deferral of Costs

- If an applicant wishes to protect his or her invention in several countries, considerable upfront costs may be incurred. By using the convention an applicant can file first in one country, for example, Canada, and defer the filing in the other Convention member countries (within the 12 months) and still claim the date of the first filing (in Canada) in those other countries. *This arrangement permits an applicant to defer the costs of the subsequent filings for some time. This may have important cash flow implications for the applicant.*

63

———————— X ——————— Y ———————————————————————➤ Time

First Filing   Subsequent Filings
& Costs   & Related Costs

To claim priority under the Paris Convention, filings Y must occur less than 12 months after filing X.

(b) Early Public Activity

- The applicant may be concerned about early public activity with the invention precluding the ability to obtain protection in some countries. *For example, some countries may not provide any grace period of public activity prior to filing an application for protection of the invention.*

- If the applicant files a patent application first, before any public activity anywhere, then by using the Convention he or she may file in the other Convention member countries (within the 12 months) and still claim the date of the first filing (in Canada) in those other countries. *This arrangement permits an applicant to backdate the subsequent filings to a date before any public activity occurred. This may permit the applicant to seek to generate some early sales or otherwise determine the market potential for the product or process incorporating or based on an invention before committing to the considerable cost of foreign filings.*

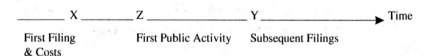

———————— X ——————— Z ———————————————— Y ——————————————➤ Time

First Filing   First Public Activity   Subsequent Filings
& Costs

The Public Activity Z may be potentially disentitling for protection in Country Y. However by claiming the filing date X the applicant has a filing date in Country Y before the disentitling public activity. To claim priority under the Paris Convention, filing Y must occur less than 12 months after filing X.

(c) Establish Priority

- The applicant may not physically be able to file all his or her applications in various countries on the same day. In some cases this may mean a competing application may obtain rights in a country if filed before the applicant's application is filed in that country. The Convention permits the applicant to claim the earliest filing date as the priority date and therefore seek to have the same priority in each country. (*See sections 2.6.3 and 3.1.1, above, and sections 27(1) and 28, Patent Act, for details on the novelty rules.*)

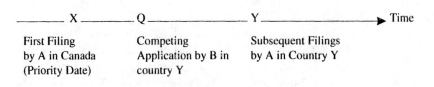

First Filing	Competing	Subsequent Filings
by A in Canada	Application by B in	by A in Country Y
(Priority Date)	country Y	

In this case without the convention applicant B has filed in Country Y before applicant A and may therefore be entitled to obtain the registration and exclusive rights in that country. By using the convention applicant A is able to backdate his or her application in Country Y to the earlier date of filing in Country X and thereby gaining priority over applicant B. Applicant A's filing Y must occur less than 12 months after filing X to claim priority under the Paris Convention.

(d) Prior Public Disclosure

- The Convention may *not work* to preserve an ability to obtain patent protection if there was prior public disclosure or otherwise the invention became available to the public before the first (priority) application is filed.

First Public Activity	First Filing	Subsequent Filings

The Public Activity Z *may* be potentially disentitling for protection in Country Y. By claiming the filing date X the applicant does <u>not</u> have a filing date in Country Y before the disentitling public activity. The applicant must still seek to file in Country Y before the expiry of any applicable grace period, if any, in that country.

3.3.2 PATENT COOPERATION TREATY

- The application of the PCT rules has received little judicial consideration as the Treaty is relatively new to Canada.

- The general principles of cost deferral and establishment of priority discussed above (sections 3.3.1(a) to (d)) also operate under the PCT but within the time frames and more complex process of the PCT.

- The PCT is administered by the World Intellectual Property Organinzation ("WIPO") and consists of two phases, an international phase and a national phase.

- Like the Paris Convention, the PCT permits the applicant to delay filing corresponding applications in other member countries. Under the PCT, the patent applicant can delay the filing of corresponding patent applications for up to 20 or even 30 months. Also like the Paris Convention, the PCT does not eliminate the need to comply with the requirements of domestic law in each country or prosecute the application in each country. Unlike the Paris Convention, the PCT may facilitate the decision making of the applicant during such prosecution and may facilitate to a degree such prosecutions of the application.

- The PCT and Paris Convention may work together. Filing under the PCT does not preclude the applicant from claiming rights under the Paris Convention.

- There are fewer member countries of the PCT than of the Paris Convention. Check to see if the countries your client wants to file in are members of the PCT. (See Appendix J for a list of member countries.) *The PCT works particularly well with applications filed under the European Patent Treaty. Note that some countries are not members of either treaty and the convention approach may not be used in such countries.*

- *Always review the domestic law of the country in which you seek to file.*

- *Always review the treaty status of the country in which you seek to file.*

- *If in doubt, get help!*

- *As with the Paris Convention, the PCT may not work to pre-serve an ability to obtain patent protection if there was prior public disclosure or otherwise the invention became available to the public before the first (priority) application is filed.*

(a) The International Phase

- The international phase begins with the filing of a single patent application in a PCT member country's "receiving office". This filing permits the applicant to designate other PCT member countries to which the filing shall relate.

- *Note that the designation of countries in excess of ten does not require a further designation fee. Note however that designation of all countries may result in costs arising in that country as the PCT application moves to the national phase unless the designation is revoked.*

- This international application may be in English, French or another official language of the PCT. The international fees are paid once and there is no need at this stage to be concerned about the formal requirements of each designated country's patent office.

- Unlike the Paris Convention, there is no need to provide each country's patent office with original drawings or certified copies of the priority application.

- The specific requirements of form and procedure are described in the PCT Applicant's Guide published by WIPO, however, generally the international patent application consists of:

  ° a request;

  ° a description;

  ° a claim or claims;

    ° one or more drawings (as necessary to understand the invention); and

    ° an abstract.

- The international application is processed by the "receiving office". A search is carried out by one of the "International Searching Authorities" of patent records of several major patent offices and an international search report is then prepared.

- The international search report and the application are published by the International Bureau of the WIPO 18 months after the priority date. *Note that this publication will affect the novelty of the invention for any subsequent patent applications.*

- The search report and the application are transmitted to each of the national patent offices designated by the applicant by the International Bureau of the WIPO. *This would begin the national phase of the PCT.*

- By use of the PCT an applicant may file first in one country, say, for example, Canada, and defer the specific filing costs in the other PCT member countries which have been designated for up to 20 months and still claim the date of the first filing (in Canada) in those other countries. *This arrangement permits an applicant to defer the costs of the translations, filing fees and related costs required in each designated country for some time. This may have important cash flow implications for the applicant.*

- A simplified example of how this deferral works (without a request for an international preliminary examination) is shown below:

X	Y		Time
0	18	20	(months)
First Filing & Costs	Search Report	Publication	Commerce National Phase & Related Costs

The PCT permits the applicant to claim the priority of filing X for 20 months after filing X. Note the publication of the application and search report at 18 months and its impact on subsequent filings.

(b) Preliminary Examination Report

- If the applicant wishes, he or she can request an international preliminary examination. This has the effect of delaying the entry into the national phase an additional ten (10) months for a total deferral of 30 months. Countries designated in the PCT application and in which the applicant has requested a preliminary examination report are said to be "elected States".

- The request for an international preliminary examination must be made within 19 months of the priority filing date. The examination will be carried out by an "International Preliminary Examining Authority" designated under the PCT.

- The main purposes of the international preliminary examination are to formulate a preliminary and non-binding opinion on whether or not the invention appears to be novel, to satisfy requirements of utility and whether there appears to be an inventive step (*i.e.*, it is non-obvious).

- This may assist the client in reviewing the merits of incurring future filing expenses in a case where the report is negative on the prospects of patentability. Obviously, you should review the report with your client and the patent agent.

- The report is typically received 28 months after the filing date of the application. This gives the applicant two months to review the opinion in the report before the application proceeds to the national phase.

- The international preliminary examination report is provided to the applicant. It is a confidential document and will not be provided to a third party unless the applicant expressly so authorizes. *While the applicant does not have to respond to the international preliminary examination report, in*

69

some cases it may be strategically useful to do so. Discuss these issues with the patent agent.

- Like the international search report, the international preliminary examination report, if provided to the examiner, is not binding on the national patent offices.

- The two main requirements to request an international preliminary examination report (and thereby benefit from the ten-month additional deferral) are:

  ° the applicant must be a resident or national of a country bound by Chapter II of the PCT; and

  ° the international application must have been filed with the receiving office of that country.

- The major effects of requesting an international preliminary examination are:

  ° the entry of the application into the national phase is delayed up to a further ten months (for a maximum total deferral of 30 months); and

  ° the applicant receives a report which addresses the substance of the application and may aid the applicant in determining whether or not to proceed, whether to seek to amend the application and the like. This information is acquired before the onset of the national phase and the applicant's requirement to incur substantial national filing fees, translation costs and the like.

- A simplified example of how this deferral works with a request for an international preliminary examination is shown below:

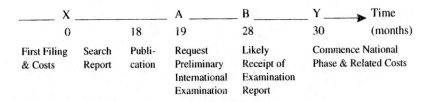

X			A	B	Y →	Time
0	18	19	28	30		(months)
First Filing & Costs	Search Report	Publi- cation	Request Preliminary International Examination	Likely Receipt of Examination Report	Commence National Phase & Related Costs	

The PCT permits the applicant to claim the priority of filing X for 30 months after filing X. The request (A) must be filed before the 19th month after filing X. The report (B) is provided to the applicant before the entry into the national phase. Note the publication of the application and search report at 18 months and its impact on subsequent filings.

(c) The National Phase

- When the application enters the national phase the applicant must:

  ° pay national (or regional) filing fees;

  ° provide any translations of the application if required by the national patent office; and

  ° appoint a local patent agent, where required, to prosecute the national application.

- Depending on the commercial prospects for the invention and the results of the international search report and, as applicable, the international preliminary examination report, the applicant may choose not to proceed in some designated countries and therefore not incur the national costs associated with that country.

- Each national patent office will apply its own rules and procedure to the application. The application is prosecuted in each national (or regional) patent office.

- Both the international search report and the international preliminary examination report are not binding on the national patent offices. The reports may however be accorded respect and considered by the national patent examiner.

(d) Summary

- A simplified example of how the PCT works, including a request for the optional international preliminary examination, is shown below:

International Phase					National Phase		
X	Z	A	B	C	D	Y	Time
0	12		18	19	28	30	(months)
First Filing & Costs	Paris Convention Deadline	Search Report	Publi- cation	Request Examination	Report Received	Commence National Phase & Related Costs	

The PCT permits the applicant to claim the priority of filing X for up to 30 months after filing X. The applicant designates those PCT member Countries in which he or she wishes to secure patent protection on filing X.

The applicant must review patent protection in non-PCT and non-Paris Convention Countries or other situations where an immediate filing may be required at the time the priority application (X) is filed.

The applicant may wish to file corresponding patent applications in non-PCT Countries or non-designated PCT Countries which are members of the Paris Convention. This must be done before the expiry of 12 months (Z) after the priority application (X) was filed.

The international search report (A) is published (B) 18 months after the application is filed (X).

The request for an international preliminary examination (C) (optional) must be filed before the 19th month after filing X.

The report arising from the international preliminary examination (D) (optional) is provided to the applicant typically nine months after the request and therefore before the entry into the national phase.

Note the publication of the application and search report at 18 months and its impact on subsequent filings.

- *Note that the example above presumes no disentitling public activity occurred prior to the priority filing date (X). If such disclosures occurred then the use of the Paris Convention and PCT are affected.*

3.3.3 DOMESTIC LAW

- It is important to review the possible applicability of utilizing convention priority in making any foreign applications for protection of the invention. *Note that some countries are not members of either the PCT or the Paris Convention.*

- If there was prior public disclosure before the first (priority) application is filed you must review the domestic law of the country in which protection is sought in order to determine if protection is still possible and, if so, what the period of any deadlines for filing are.

- Patent protection must be sought in non-convention countries by reference to the domestic law and/or any bilateral treaties which the applicable country may have in place, if any.

- *If in doubt, get help!*

3.3.4 FILING PRIORITY

- Only the true inventor may make a valid application. As a result, a person who has seen another person's prior invention cannot make a valid application for a patent in relation to that invention.

- In certain cases, very similar inventions may be made independently by two or more inventors. In a dispute as to who should obtain the patent, the Patent Office will grant the patent to the person who files their application first. *(See sections 2.6.4 and 3.1.1, above, and section 28.2(1)(c), Patent Act.)*

- The U.S. priority in cases of competing patent applications is based on the first to invent. This rule is discussed in more detail in section 2.11, above.

- It is important to file an application for a patent in relation to an invention as soon as practical so as to establish as early a filing date as possible in the event of conflicting applications.

- The operation of convention priority claims by a foreign applicant may permit the foreign applicant to have priority for obtaining a patent for the invention in Canada. (*See sections 28.1 and 28.2, Patent Act, and sections 2.6.4, 3.3.1(c), above, and 6.4, below.*)

- *Always review the domestic law of the country in which you seek to file.*

- *Always review the treaty status of the country in which you seek to file.*

- *If in doubt, get help!*

3.4 FUTURE DISCLOSURES

- Until the application for a patent in the United States Patent and Trademark Office is granted, the invention is not available to the public from the U.S. office.

- In Canada and most other countries, the patent application will be laid open to the public 18 months after the application is filed (or the priority date).

- If the invention itself has not been made public then the applicant may be able to continue to maintain trade secret protection over the details of the invention until the applicant decides to make the application public or it is laid open to the public by operation of the *Patent Act.*

- In some cases, certain confidential dealings with the invention (which do not result in the invention being made available to the public) may be maintained under obligations of confidence through use of a non-disclosure agreement.

- *Sample non-disclosure agreements are attached in the Appendices K and L.* Considerations in use of such arrangements are found at Appendix M.

3.5 INFRINGEMENT

3.5.1 RISKS OF INFRINGING

- A patent provides a bundle of monopoly rights to the patent holder. It is an infringement to do anything which only the patent holder has the right to do (*see section 2.5.2, above, for a description of those rights*).

- The applicant should always consider whether or not there is a risk of infringement in respect of the invention. Also consider the possibility of infringement of other intellectual property rights in respect of technology.

- A common remedy sought by a plaintiff is an interim injunction restraining the infringer from carrying on further infringements and seeking seizure of any infringing goods. *Such a remedy may assist in preserving the status quo rather than requiring the plaintiff to endure continued infringements for several years until a trial can finally address the issue.*

- The *Patent Act provides a number of civil remedies for patent infringement including injunction, damages, an accounting for profits and delivery up of infringing goods (sections 54, 55 and 57, Patent Act). The remedies obtained depend on the circumstances of the case.*

- Infringing activity in the field of patents requires proof by the plaintiff that:

  ° without the consent of the owner of a patent, a defendant did make, use or sell,

  ° without lawful authority or defence,

    ° a product or process (as applicable) coming within the claims of the plaintiff's valid unexpired patent.

- An action must be commenced within six years of the infringment complained of (see section 55.01 *Patent Act.*)

3.5.2 OPTIONS IF RISK OF INFRINGEMENT

- If a technology your client wishes to use may be infringing, your client may consider the following options:

    ° the client should not carry out the infringing activity;

    ° the client should consider obtaining a licence to use, reproduce, *etc.*, the prior rights which may relate to the technology;

    ° the client should consider the risks and consequences of carrying out the infringing activity;

    ° the client should consider whether or not a technology may be created which is substantially different or otherwise not infringing of the prior rights;

    ° the client should consider whether or not there is a basis to attack the existence of the other party's rights (*see sections 3.5.3, 3.5.4 and 3.5.5, below*); or

    ° if the potential plaintiff's conduct may be found to be an abuse of his or her patent rights it may be possible to obtain a compulsory licence or other relief under section 65 of the *Patent Act.*

3.5.3 CHALLENGES TO VALIDITY

- Your searches or research may disclose prior art which was not tested during the prosecution of the prior patent, disentitling prior public conduct with the invention, or other bases on which to challenge the claims in the patent.

- A patent or claim in a patent may be declared invalid or void by the Federal Court, which has exclusive jurisdiction to impeach a claim in a patent, either at the instance of the Attorney General or by any interested party (section 60, *Patent Act*).

- The validity or enforceability of a patent is often also raised as a defence to an infringement action. Such action may be brought in either the Federal Court or in a provincial court which has the applicable jurisdiction for the remedies your client may seek (section 54, *Patent Act*).

3.5.4 PROTESTS

- Your client may be concerned that a patent application has not been or may not be tested against certain published prior art, such as prior patents, laid open patent applications or other printed publications. In such cases he or she may wish to consider filing a protest to bring to the attention of the Patent Office examiner the published prior art.

- Any person may file prior art consisting of printed publications, patents and laid open patent applications with the Commissioner of Patents in relation to a patent application. (See Rule 10, Patent Rules, and section 34.1, *Patent Act*.)

- A person filing a protest must explain the pertinency of the prior art (section 34.1(2), *Patent Act*).

- The Commissioner of Patents will acknowledge receipt of the protest but the party filing the protest will get no notice of any action taken on it. (See Rule 10, Patent Rules.)

- The person filing a protest may need to do further periodic searches of the patent file to determine what action has been taken on the protest, if any. *Note that the person filing the protest does not have an opportunity to rebut arguments the patent applicant may use to overcome the protest.*

- A person considering filing a protest must consider whether the limited role available to him or her in a protest justifies taking the action.

- *Note that only published prior art may be considered. It is not possible to bring evidence of prior disentitling disclosures or other grounds upon which the validity of the patent may be challenged. On the other hand, until a patent issues no court challenge may be launched.*

3.5.5 RE-EXAMINATION

- Your client may be concerned that an issued patent was not tested against certain published prior art. In such cases he or she may wish to consider requesting re-examination of the patent in light of the published prior art.

- If re-examination is requested by a person other than the patentee then the request must be filed in duplicate.

- A person requesting re-examination must explain the pertinency of the prior art (section 48.1(2), *Patent Act*).

- See sections 48.1 to 48.5, *Patent Act*, for the procedure before the re-examination board and appeals.

- *Note that only published prior art may be considered. It is not possible to bring evidence of prior disentitling disclosures or other grounds upon which the validity of the patent may be challenged. For these reasons where a patentee uncovers possible pertinent published prior art the patentee may wish to request re-examination himself or herself and seek to control the arguments made to the examiner.*

- A decision of the re-examination board may be appealed to the Federal Court of Canada.

4

PREPARATION

4.1 INTRODUCTION

4.1.1 THE DECISION TO SEARCH

- Since an invention must satisfy certain requirements of novelty (*see sections 2.6.3 and 3.1.1, above*) a patentability search may disclose the existence of any similar inventions.

- Given the novelty rules, if time and resources are not limited, your client should search the patent records of every patent office and also conduct comprehensive searches for unpatented inventions or other relevant materials in the art or trade relating to the invention throughout the world. If such extensive searching may not be commercially feasible for your client you should discuss with the client how to and where to carry out searches to maximize the benefit at the minimum cost.

- It is always prudent to conduct a search of the Patent Office to determine whether or not a particular client's invention is infringing on the rights of any third party.

- A patent search may also identify whether an assignment of a patent or a licence has been registered.

- Note that commonly a novelty search is conducted in order to assess patentability. A separate analysis and search may be conducted to assess infringement risk, if desired. Ascertain if your client's search addresses novelty, identification of infringement risk or both.

- Inform your client of the risks in not carrying out comprehensive searches. Those risks include:

  ° The client's invention or a part of it may be infringing on the rights of a third party which are not identified. This risk may be mitigated to some extent by doing searches in the countries where the client wishes to use, manufacture or sell products or processes incorporating the invention.

  ° The client's invention may not be patentable due to the existence of relevant prior art that either renders the client's invention not new or obvious in light of that prior art.

- *Always review the prospect of searching in any country in which you seek to file a patent application or use the technology.*

- *If in doubt, get help!*

(a) Patent Office Records

- The records of the Patent Office may be searched manually in the Patent Office in Hull, Quebec. These records comprise over 1 million Canadian patents and over 5 million U.S. patents which are available for searching.

- Except in the case of section 11 searches (*see below*), the staff at the Patent Office will not carry out the searches for you.

- Printed copies of patents can be obtained as follows:

  ° For patents prior to patent number 445,930, from the Patent Office.

  ° For patents from patent number 445,930 on, from Micromedia Limited at 165 Hôtel-de-Ville, Hull, Quebec, J8X 3X2.

(b) Library Records

- Many public and university libraries also contain some patent information including the subject index, class schedules and class listings providing lists of Canadian patents in some areas or fields on microfiche and in some cases on CD-ROM.

(c) Electronic Searches

- Electronic searches of the Dialog Information Retrieval Services or other databases may also be useful. Some of the important patent databases available on Dialog are:

  ° *U.S. Patents Fulltext* — This database is produced by Dialog and provides access to 1.4 million patents issued by the United States Patent and Trademark Office since 1974 with partial coverage from 1971 to 1973.

  ° *Claims/U.S. Patents* — This database provides access to 1.7 million patents issued by the United States Patent and Trademark Office since 1950.

  ° *Claims/Re-assignment & Re-examination* — This database provides information on U.S. patents which have been re-examined or re-assigned. The database has about 35,000 records and covers re-assigned patents from 1980 and re-examined patents from 1981.

  ° *Claims/Reference* — This database provides a dictionary index to the subject classification used in the CLAIMS family of databases. The database has about 150,000 records.

  ° *Claims/Citation* — This database contains patent references which have been cited by patent examiners against U.S. patent applications. The database has about 3.3 million records.

° *INPATDOC/Family and Legal Status* — This database is provided by the International Patent Documentation Center, Vienna, and contains a listing of patents issued in 56 countries and various patent organizations. The database provides access to approximately 7.7 million patents. A useful feature of this database is that it contains information on priority applications, priority dates and corresponding applications filed in other countries.

° *World Patent Index* — This database is provided by Derwent Publications, Ltd. and provides access to approximately 7 million patent documents describing about 3 million inventions. Patent families are also described.

° *European Patents Fulltext* — This database provides access to all European patent applications and granted European patents published since the opening of the European Patent Office in 1978. There are presently about 600,000 records.

° *Chinese Patent Abstracts in English* — This database is produced by the Patent Documentation Service Centre of the People's Republic of China ("PRC") and provides access to all patents published in the PRC by the Patent Office since April 1, 1985. The database has about 1,500 records.

• Other electronic sources and databases include:

° Thomson Professional Publishing's *Canadian Law On-Line*, providing on-line access to the *Canadian Abridgement*, providing digests of case law and to history and judicial treatments of the case law.

° QL Systems Ltd.'s *QuickLaw* and West Publishing's *Westlaw* for case law which may have interpreted the patent claims. *Westlaw* also provides a noting up service and secondary materials.

° Infomart Dialog Ltd.'s *Infomart Law On-Line* which provides statutory materials, case law, a noting up service and secondary materials.

° Mead DataCentral's *Lexis* which provides mostly American (but some Canadian and Commonwealth) cases, a noting up service, statutes and secondary materials or which provides news and other secondary materials.

° The Globe and Mail's *Info Globe* which provides business and general news materials.

• In addition, consider reviewing any automated or paper-based databases of industry newsletters, journals and materials applicable to the industry to which your client's (or a third party's) invention relates.

• Certain Canadian patent files are available and may be searched on the Internet. In addition useful information and forms are available on-line. See <http://www.cipo.ca> for the Canadian Intellectual Property Office web site.

• Certain United States patent files, U.S. Forms and information may be obtained at <http://www.uspto.org>.

• A variety of companies, organizations and other countries also post patent information on the Internet. The searcher must review the scope, accuracy, timeliness and coverage of the information available from such sources. Examples of some such other web sites include:

° A variety of U.K. patent information is available from the Derwent Patent web site, available at <http://www.derwent.uk>.

° Certain European Patent office patent files, forms and information may be obtained at <http://www.epo.co.at>.

° One may search European patent, Japanese, WO and other patent materials using the esp@cenet service pro-

vided through the European Patent Office. See
<http://www.epo.co.at/espacenet/info/access.htm> for
details on how to access this service and the languages
supported. Some full text documents are available in PDF
format from this service.

° Micropatent provides a commercial patent search service
including full text of U.S. Patents issued since 1976. See
<http://www.micropat.com> for details.

° Certain Canadian patent files may be obtained at the
PATSCAN service hosted by the University of British Co-
lumbia. See <http://www.library.ubc.ca> for details.

- You might also consider using the IPC:Class (International
Patent Classification and Linguistic Advanced Search System) patent classification system produced by the World Intellectual Property Organization. *IPC:Class is available on
CD-ROM.*

(d) Other Sources

- Depending on the nature of the invention, you should also
consider searching the records of the Industrial Design Office. While an industrial design registration protects only
aesthetic features of the design (not useful features) there
may be similar designs which were filed in the Industrial Design Office. In such cases the owner may have sought to
protect the aesthetic features of a design or invention under
the industrial design system.

- Consider searching the records of the United States Patent
and Trademark Office. More Canadian inventors file patent
applications in the U.S. Patent and Trademark Office than in
the Canadian Patent Office (*see section 2.11, above*). The
files of the United States Patent and Trademark Office are
also well organized and indexed.

4.1.2 TYPES OF SEARCHES

- There are many specialized searches which may be carried out. Some of the more important types of searches are described below.

(a) Locate Searches

- A search may be conducted to locate a specific invention or patent, all of the patents made by certain inventors or all registrations or licences owned by or in the name of certain parties and which have been registered in the Patent Office.

- An identifier must be known to carry out such a search. *For example, you might search the name of the inventor, the name of the owner or the patent registration number.*

- It is possible to identify whether a patent application has been filed in the Canadian Patent Office which is a counterpart to a patent issued in another country even before the patent application is laid open to the public. In such a case you must make a special request under section 11 of the *Patent Act* and provide the Commissioner with:

  ° the name of the inventor, if known;

  ° the title of the invention;

  ° the country in which the patent was granted;

  ° the number and date of the patent granted in that country; and

  ° a fee (*see Appendix G for the Fee Schedule*).

- See Rule 11, Patent Rules.

(b) Field Searches

- A search might be carried out to identify all patents in a cer-tain field. *For example, a inventor might wish to see the pat-ents of competitors directed at the same problem as the inventor's invention.*

- This type of search may provide an indication of who is ac-tive in this field and the lines of inquiry they have pursued in the past. This type of search may also permit you to identify potential competitors or licensees.

- To initiate such a search you will need to study the descrip-tions used in the Patent Office for the class or classes of in-ventions of interest to your client. It may be that a variety of descriptive terms might be applicable. Once those are de-termined your search may be facilitated.

(c) Patentability Search

- A patentability search seeks to identify any issued patents or laid open patent applications which may be relevant to the invention your client wishes to protect.

- Such a search may assist in determining whether the inven-tion appears to be new, and to a limited extent whether the invention appears to be obvious based on the prior art lo-cated.

- In order to carry out such a search you must determine those elements or key features of the client's invention.

- A patentability search will typically not identify infringement of third party rights.

(d) Infringement Search

- An infringement search seeks to identify any issued patents or other rights (such as protected topographies, registered industrial designs, the possible claims in laid open patent applications, *etc.*) which may be infringed by features of the client's invention.

- Such a search may assist the client in assessing any risk of infringement. It may also be useful in clearing the risk of infringement for new products or processes.

- In order to carry out such a search you need to identify each feature of your client's invention and carry out a search for prior patents and/or other registrations which relate to each such feature. This is very different than a novelty or patentability search which focuses only on the inventive features of the invention.

- If you identify a possible prior patent or other right in another jurisdiction then you should carry out a search for counterpart applications which may have been filed in Canada, if any.

- Since Canada is a smaller market place, many foreign inventors do not file patent applications in Canada. In such cases and where the novelty rules would prevent subsequent filings by such inventors (see section 28.2(1)(d), *Patent Act*), that inventor may have no patent protection for the invention in Canada.

(e) Validity Search

- A validity search tends to be a more extensive search. It addresses the facts which might affect the validity of a issued patent.

- Examples of such searches include:

  ° searches directed at whether the invention was made available to the public more than one year before the application was filed;

  ° searches to find similarity to other prior published inventions or issued patents; or

° searches to find similarity to any prior publication in industry or trade journals.

- In order to carry out such a search you need to analyze each
claim of the invention in question and carry out a search for
prior art in industry or trade materials, prior patent and/or
other registrations and prior unissued patent applications
which relate to the elements of each such claim.

- A useful starting point is to obtain a copy of the file wrapper
(the filing and prosecution history) of the patent in question
from the Patent Office.

- In each case you need identify when relevant prior art was
made known to the public and compare it with the filing date
of the invention under study.

- You might also conduct searches to identify:

  ° if the proper inventors were named in the application;

  ° if the application was properly filed;

  ° if all formalities were complied with;

  ° if any material allegations in the petition are untrue; and

  ° such other technical bases for attacks on the validity of a
  patent.

4.1.3 LIMITATIONS OF SEARCHES

- Except as noted in section 4.1.2(b) (section 11 searches),
above, searches in the Patent Office will locate only issued
patents or patent applications laid open to the public.

- Applications for a patent are laid open to the public for
searching purposes 18 months after the filing date or priority
date, whichever is first (section 10, *Patent Act*).

- In some cases a patent or patent application may have been registered but for clerical reasons may not yet be available for searching. Missing files, errors in indices and typographical errors may also limit the completeness of a search.

- Searches of electronic databases are based on use of key words. Errors in the key word either by the searcher or in the database may affect the search result. Further, there is no consistency in the use of descriptive words or key words by patent agents. As a result your search strategy should consider alternative ways to describe the particular feature in which you are interested. *This is particularly important for patents which may be located in different countries with different language usage or terms of art.*

- Generally more sophisticated search tools are available on the commercial databases than on the Internet.

- It is possible to identify whether a patent application has been filed in the Canadian Patent Office which is a counterpart to a patent issued in another country. *(See section 4.1.2(b), above.)*

- Advise your client on the limitations of the searches and that a search result may not be complete or accurate.

- *See also the cautions in section 4.1.1, above, regarding where searches are carried out.*

4.2 PATENT AGENTS

4.2.1 WHAT IS A PATENT AGENT?

A patent agent is a professional trained in patent law and practice who can assist an inventor in the preparation, filing and prosecution of a patent application. Patent agents are regulated by the Commissioner of Patents. In addition, most patent agents are members of the Patent and Trade-mark Institute of Canada (PTIC) which represents registered patent and trade-mark agents. The PTIC provides numerous courses to assist in becoming a patent (or trademark) agent or for continuing education. Contact either the Commissioner of Patents or the PTIC for information on becoming a patent agent.

- Only the inventor or a registered patent agent (or an associate registered patent agent) appointed by the inventor may prosecute the patent application before the Patent Office (Rule 20(1), Patent Rules).

- Non-resident patent agents must appoint a Canadian associate patent agent to prosecute the application in Canada (Rule 21(1), Patent Rules).

- A patent agent is not required to be a lawyer. Of course, if your patent agent is not a lawyer, the patent agent cannot provide you or your client with legal advice. Most patent agents have, however, a background or training in engineering or science. This background tends to aid in understanding more complex inventions.

- In working with a patent agent, keep in mind that communications with a patent agent are *not* privileged: see *Lumonics Research Ltd. v. Gould* (1983), 70 C.P.R. (2d) 11 (Fed. C.A.). Law reform efforts may change this in the future.

- Most patent agents work in groups and therefore may be able to provide their clients complementary skills and experiences. *For example, one or several patent agent(s) may have training, experience and skills in chemical, biological and/or pharmaceutical applications and other agent(s) may have skills, background and training in electronic or algorithm applications.*

- *You may wish to enquire about the technical strengths and experience of the patent agents you work with.*

4.2.2 MANAGING THE PATENT AGENT

- Some of the important factors which may assist you in working well with a patent agent include:

  ° a clear understanding of the patent agent's fees and basis on which charges are incurred;

° a clear understanding of who will pay the patent agent's fees, *i.e.*, you, your firm or the client directly;

° a clear understanding of the role the patent agent will perform;

° timely information and reporting on work done by the patent agent;

° availability and accessability of the patent agent;

° the ability of the patent agent to remain flexible and open-minded in characterizing the invention — *if the patent agent is too rigid, technical or inflexible your client's invention may be characterized too narrowly and potential rights may be lost.* The patent agent's ego should not be or become a barrier to preparation of a strong patent application;

° the ability of the patent agent to work carefully and in a timely manner so that your client may obtain the earliest possible filing (and priority) date; and

° how well the patent agent, you and your client interact — *a personality conflict may adversely affect the ability to properly protect your client's interests.*

• Your responsibilities in working with the patent agent include:

° ensuring clear instructions and directions are communicated;

° providing timely responses to information requests;

° advising of any particular issues or special circumstances of the applicant and in particular if the applicant is a "small entity" (*see section 4.4.8, below*) and on ownership issues (*see section 2.7, above*);

- ° managing the client relationship so that your client has a realistic appreciation of what to expect (and what not to expect) from the patent application and prosecution process;

- ° facilitating good interaction between the patent agent and the inventor; and

- ° addressing the payment of your fees and the patent agent's fees (if billed to you or your firm).

- *Where you do not know your client well and have no reasonable assurances as to how the fees will be paid, a retainer arrangement is strongly advised!*

- If your client's application is rejected by the examiner, your client may lose interest in pursuing the application. It may be difficult to collect the fees incurred to date. The same issue may arise with adverse search results.

- The Patent Office maintains a list of current registered patent agents. You may also identify a patent agent from:

  - ° past positive experience or recommendations from trusted colleagues;

  - ° listings in sources such as Martindale Hubbell, the Yellow Pages®, industry directories and specialized industry publications;

  - ° Web sites including <http:www.//www.cipo.gc.ca>; or

  - ° personal connections such as persons met at conferences, *etc.*

- *Remember you must be able to work closely with the patent agent.*

4.2.3 MANAGING FOREIGN FILINGS

- If foreign filings are based on the priority application you will need to:

° have a copy of the priority application as filed;

° depending on the requirements of the other country, have a certified copy of the filing materials; and

° typically you or your client will need to appoint agents in the foreign country.

• Important factors in establishing a successful working relationship with a foreign agent include:

° the specific filing requirements in the particular country;

° a clear understanding of the patent agent's fees and basis on which charges are incurred;

° a clear understanding of who will pay the patent agent's fees, you, your firm or your client;

° a clear understanding of the role the patent agent will perform;

° timely information and reporting on work done by the patent agent for the client; and

° availability and accessability of the patent agent for advice.

• In many countries a translation of the application into the local language may be required. You should discuss access, availability and the costs for such translation services with the foreign agent.

• You can locate foreign patent agents from a variety of sources including:

° past positive experience or recommendations from trusted colleagues;

° listings in sources such as Martindale Hubbell, specialized industry publications, *etc.*;

° personal connections such as persons met at conferences, *etc.*;

° information from web sites; or

° recommendations from your Canadian patent agent.

• It is most common that your Canadian patent agent has a
relationship with a foreign patent agent that they have confidence in. You may wish to ask your Canadian patent agent
about their experience with the foreign patent office.

• *Your foreign agent is a part of your client's team and can be a
useful source of information regarding the law and practice in
the applicable country. You will generally get as much out of
the relationship as you put into it.*

4.2.4 HOW TO BECOME A PATENT AGENT

• Except for Patent Office staff, to write the examination to become a registered patent agent you must:

° notify the Commissioner of Patents in the applicable time
that you wish to sit for the examination;

° pay the fee set out in Schedule II (presently $200) (see
Rule 15(2), Patent Rules);

° reside in Canada;

° have been employed for a period of at least 12 months in
the area of patent law including the preparation and prosecution of patent applications; and

° file with the Commissioner an affidavit setting out the applicable experience and responsibilities (see Rule 12(2),
Patent Rules).

- The Patent and Trade-mark Institute of Canada provides courses which may assist in preparation for the examination.

- McGill University provides a summer course on Canadian patent law in conjunction with the Patent and Trade-mark Institute of Canada which may assist in preparation for the examination.

- A reasonable basis for preparation may be to:

  ° obtain experience working with capable patent agents for a sufficient period to gain an appreciation of patent agency practice and experience on patent applications in a variety of fields;

  ° study the law and cases applicable to patent agency practice;

  ° take the courses available through the Patent and Trade-mark Institute of Canada, *etc.*; and

  ° take courses on patent law and patent agency practice available elsewhere including in the United States.

4.3 CLIENT'S CANDOUR

The relationship between a lawyer and client is a fiduciary relationship. An obligation of confidence is included as part of the lawyer's obligations to the client. It is suggested the relationship between the patent agent and client is also a fiduciary relationship since it too is based on a requirement of high trust.

- Your client should be encouraged to be completely candid with you and the patent agent regarding the invention. This is of critical importance in a number of key areas such as:

  ° Issues of inventorship — Who truly are the inventors? Did the client make any inventive contribution?

  ° Issues of prior disclosure or making available to the public including publications, displays, sale or offer of sale, *etc.*

- ° Issues of knowledge of prior art.

- ° Issues relating to unsuccessful tests, early trials, *etc.*

- It is important that your client gives you and the patent agent full, truthful and complete information.

- Some inventors may make it difficult for you to get the full story. They may be unable or unwilling to communicate clearly or in a logical manner or may, intentionally or inadvertently, be unwilling to cooperate for any number of reasons. In such cases, you and the patent agent will have to assist the inventor in giving a complete disclosure.

- *The inventor is the expert on his or her invention. If he or she does not give you and the patent agent full disclosure then you cannot properly advise on the client's legal rights and the validity and/or scope of the patent application may be adversely affected.*

4.4 INITIAL APPLICATION

- In preparing an application for a patent in Canada, you should consider, among other things:

  - ° applicability of patent protection to the technology or thing in question;

  - ° the interrelationship of the *Patent Act* and other forms of intellectual property protection and whether a patent is the appropriate or only form of protection;

  - ° the identities, nationality, domicile and legal status of all inventors of the invention and their relationship to the party claiming title to the invention;

  - ° the basis upon which the party claiming title to the invention claims such title (whether by operation of law or by agreement or otherwise);

° whether the work has been "published" or made available to the public, the date of said publication and the implications of publication on any rights;

° whether there are several inventions which should be the basis of separate applications;

° applicability and requirements of international treaty or convention provisions;

° existence, scope and terms of any underlying licensed rights to portions of the invention;

° the correct spelling of the name of the invention, any terms of art, the inventors and owners;

° the countries in which production is sought; and

° your client's commercial requirements in order for exploitation of the invention.

• *The inventor is the expert in the field of his or her invention. You must assist the inventor to articulate the essence, scope and elements of the invention so that a proper and complete disclosure may be prepared.*

4.4.1 ELEMENTS OF A PATENT APPLICATION

• In Canada a patent application consists of the following parts (*further details of these elements are discussed below*):

° a specification, which includes:

— a detailed description of the invention; and

— the claims;

° drawings; and

° an abstract.

- In addition, the application is usually accompanied by several other documents, depending on the circumstances of the case, such as:

  ° a petition;

  ° an assignment;

  ° an appointment of agent;

  ° a declaration of status; and

  ° a request for examination.

- These documents are described below. Note that different rules may be applicable to patent applications filed before October 1, 1996. See the Patent Rules for transition provisions.

4.4.2 PREPARING THE ABSTRACT

- The abstract is a brief technical description of the disclosure which illustrates the utility of the invention and how the invention may be distinguished from other inventions (see Rule 78(4), Patent Rules). it is usually prepared after the specification so that the abstract more accurately reflects the essence of the invention.

- The abstract is also used for searching purposes in many database systems.

- *Do not use the abstract to determine the scope or extent of the monopoly granted under a patent (see Rule 79(1), Patent Rules). The claims define the scope and extent of the patent monopoly.*

- *A sample abstract is provided in the former Form 24 of the Patent Forms (see Appendix F).*

4.4.3 PREPARING THE SPECIFICATION

- The specification is made up of a description and the claims.

- A useful technique to prepare a first or preliminary detailed description is to answer the questions outlined in parts (a) to (c), below. The inventor must add to such answers a detailed explanation of how the invention works.

- The preliminary detailed description will be of considerable assistance to the patent agent in preparing the application. Often the more complete and detailed the preliminary detailed description is, the less expense will be incurred in having the patent agent prepare the application.

- As the inventor is the expert on the invention, he or she should be responsible for preparation of the preliminary detailed description. You may be able to assist the inventor in being as complete and accurate as possible. You may also be able to help identify some of the benefits of the invention and possible variations or substitutions of parts of the invention.

- *Examples of formal detailed descriptions are attached in Appendices F and H.*

(a)   What is the Problem Being Solved?

- Most inventions solve practical problems. Defining the problem being solved aids in defining the art or industry in which the invention may be assessed.

- The solution of a practical problem serves to satisfy the requirement of utility *(see section 2.6.2, above)*.

- *See the sample patent attached in Appendix H showing one way to describe the problem being solved by that invention. See also the former Form 24 of the Patent Forms in Appendix F.*

(b) How Have Others Tried to Solve the Problem?

- The client should describe, as completely as he or she knows, how others in the industry or art have tried to solve the same problem.

- While the client is not obligated to do searches to improve his or her knowledge, searches may assist in determining whether problems will be encountered in the prosecution of the application. (*See section 4.1 on searches.*) Moreover, the description of what others have sought to do in solving the problem serves to begin to define the prior art the invention will be tested against.

- *In the sample patent in Appendix H see how the prior art is identified as efforts by others to solve the problem. See also a further example in the former Form 24 of the Patent Forms in Appendix F.*

- Identify all prior art known including:

  ° any relevant patents (*i.e.*, uncovered in conducting searches, *etc.*);

  ° relevant technical articles, papers, conference proceedings and the like; and

  ° any relevant technology sold or made available by third parties.

- In each case provide sufficient information to completely identify the prior art source and where possible provide copies of the prior art.

(c) What Makes the Invention Different from what Others have done Before?

- Describe what advantages the invention has over the prior art. *See section 1.4.5, above, for a sample list of possible advantages.*

- Since to be an invention the client's technology must both be new (*see section 2.6.3, above*) and not be obvious to a person skilled in the art (*see section 2.6.4, above*), distinguishing the prior art is very important.

- The advantages of the invention over the prior art are also very important since these advantages will be used to define the claims of the invention and hence the extent and scope of the monopoly rights obtained.

- *See Appendices F and H for samples of the specific advantages of the invention over the prior art.*

4.4.4 DETAILED DESCRIPTION

- The detailed description is one of the most important and yet difficult parts of the patent application. The purpose of the detailed description is to set out the invention in sufficient detail that a person skilled in the art could use, make or practice the invention. As a result the detailed description of the invention must be sufficiently complete. The inventor is the expert on how the description is used, practised or made. *It is very important for the inventor to spend sufficient time and effort in this aspect. It will ultimately help reduce the work and costs of the patent agent.*

- Typically the inventor will prepare a preliminary detailed description of the invention. The inventor and patent agent will normally develop a more thorough and extensive detailed description through an iterative process. The inventor can save time and money through his or her efforts in providing a more complete and extensive detailed description of the invention.

- Theoretically the detailed description can assume the knowledge that should be available to a person skilled in the art. However as a practical matter neither the examiner in the Patent Office nor a judge who later has to interpret the invention will necessarily have that knowledge. As a result, if in doubt, provide a more complete description. This may serve to avoid a future need to prove what the knowledge of a person skilled in the art might be.

- Such disclosure will, once the application is laid open to the public or is otherwise made publically available, preclude trade secret protection over the information disclosed.

- The following points should be noted when preparing the description:

  ° The description should focus on the invention and how the invention is made, practised or used.

  ° The description should be accurate and should relate to the drawings.

  ° The description should describe the key or principal features of the invention.

  ° The description should describe any variations or substitutions in the way the invention is made, used or practised.

  ° The description should describe all useful features of the invention.

  ° Additional technical requirements are set out in Rule 80, Patent Rules.

- The inventor should specifically describe the best mode or preferred way to practise, use or make the invention in the description. At least one practical example should be provided.

- The description should identify:

  ° the materials used to make or use the invention;

  ° any conditions on use or operation of the invention;

  ° any test results;

° any limits necessary to obtain the results expected from the invention; and

° any variations expected from use of or making the invention.

- *Note both the specific detail provided in the description and how the description is tied directly to the drawings in the sample patent set out in Appendix H.*

4.4.5 THE DRAWINGS

- The drawings are important since they provide a visual tie to the written description of the features of the invention. Drawings can also be used to show the features of the invention including variations contemplated. If the variations are such that several quite different and unrelated inventions are shown, you may need to consider separating the applications. Discuss this with the patent agent.

- Normally a draftsperson is required to prepare the drawings. Your client may have such resources in house, you may know of such a person or the patent agent may have applicable contacts. You will need to identify the cost for preparation of the formal drawings and make arrangements with the client for payment of these costs.

- In some cases the application may be filed with informal drawings such as sketches of the invention. Such drawings will not satisfy the technical requirements for the formal drawings. Formal drawings will still be required before the patent will issue.

- Any informal drawings must be sufficiently clear to illustrate each of the details of the invention. Filing with adequate informal drawings permits the client to defer the costs of preparation of the formal drawings until there may be more certainty that the patent will issue.

- Caution is urged in relying on drawings to interpret what the scope of the rights under a patent might be. The scope of the monopoly rights is defined by the claims, not the drawings.

- The rules for preparation of drawings are technical and detailed.

- All views of a drawing must be on paper that is:

  ° Either 21.6 cm x 27.9 cm or 21 cm x 29.7 cm (A4 format) (Rule 68(1), Patent Rules), and

  ° The description, claims and abstract shall have a top margin of at least 2 cm, left side margin of at least 2.5 cm, right side and bottom margin of at least 2 cm. Drawings shall have a top and left side margin of at least 2.5 cm, a right side margin of at least 1.5 cm and a bottom margin of at least 1 cm. (Rules 69(1), 69(2), Patent Rules).

- Each sheet of the drawings should be on white bond paper. There should be no other markings on such sheets except for the drawings, reference characters and legends pertaining to the drawings (Rule 30(1)(h), Patent Rules).

- The drawings must be free of creases, folds, bends or other imperfections (Rule 30(3), Patent Rules). If sent by mail, the drawings should be protected by a sheet of binders board (Rule 30(4), Patent Rules).

- The drawing must be prepared with clear, permanent black lines (Rule 82(1), Patent Rules).

- All views of a drawing should show features of the invention clearly and accurately.

- All views on the same sheet should stand in the same direction.

- Views should be numbered consecutively throughout the drawings regardless of the number of sheets of paper used (Rule 82(8), Patent Rules).

- If necessary a view can be divided between two or more sheets of paper (Rule 82(7), Patent Rules).

- Do not show views in different scales unless necessary for the clarity of the drawing (Rule 82(4), Patent Rules).

- All views of a drawing should be of sufficient scale as to be clear and should be separated by sufficient space to keep them distinct.

- Use as few section lines, lines for effect and shading lines as possible.

- All reference characters should be clear, distinct and not less than 0.32 cm in height (Rule 82(5), Patent Rules).

- Reference characters should be the same in different views (Rule 82(10), Patent Rules).

- *While applicable using older rules or drawings, see examples of formal drawings in Appendix H. Note the detailed views, perspectives and use of exploded and cut-away views to illustrate the features of the inventions.*

4.4.6 MODELS AND SAMPLES

- Do not send models or samples of the invention unless requested by the Commissioner of Patents (section 38(1), *Patent Act*).

- If models or samples are sent they should be clearly and securely marked to identify the application to which they relate (Rule 31(5), Patent Rules).

- Unless the Commissioner of Patents permits otherwise, a model should not exceed 12 inches (30 cm) on its longest side (Rule 31(2), Patent Rules).

- Samples must be provided in appropriate containers (Rule 31(3), Patent Rules).

- Dangerous substances are only to be provided in accordance with instructions provided by the Commissioner (section 38(2), *Patent Act*).

4.4.7 THE CLAIMS

- The claims describe the elements of the invention and define the monopoly the patentee seeks in the application. In interpreting the claims, the courts may look to the dictionary meaning of the words used and the meaning given in the description: see. *Baxter Travenol Laboratories of Canada Ltd. v. Cutter (Canada) Ltd.* (1983), 68 C.P.R. (2d) 179 (Fed. C.A.), leave to appeal refused (1983), 72 C.P.R. (2d) 287, 51 N.R. 238 (S.C.C.).

- There may be many inventions described in the application. Each claim is a separate invention and should define in a single sentence, as generally or as broadly as permissible, all the elements which make up the invention.

- Draft from the broadest claim (*i.e.*, with the least limitations or qualifications) to the narrowest (*i.e.*, with the greatest number of limitations or qualifications).

- Each claim seeks to define in a single sentence and as broadly as permissible the elements which make up the invention.

- There are two types of claims:

  - Independent Claims — These are claims which stand on their own. *Examples of independent claims are claims 1, 9, 15 and 16 in the example found in Appendix H. See also claim 1 in example claims A, B and C of former Form 24, Patent Forms, Appendix F.*

  - Dependent Claims — These claims qualify or add additional limitations to a prior claim. *For example, in the example found in Appendix H, claim 2 adds the further requirement of the guide member being coupled to and ro-*

tatable with the lower barrel member to the more general claim 1. See also claims 2, 3 and, as applicable, 4 in example claims A, B and C of former Form 24, Patent Forms, Appendix F.

- There are numerous technical rules regarding the proper drafting of claims. Because of the importance of the claims, involve a patent agent in the drafting of the claims. *Errors made in drafting may affect the scope, extent, validity and enforceability of the patent rights.*

- In drafting the claims care must be taken:

  ° to describe the elements of the invention as broadly as possible to capture the greatest permissible scope and extent of the monopoly; and

  ° not to claim features which are part of the prior art and therefore outside the scope of the invention.

- *Note that special claim language may be required to obtain applicable protection for certain types of inventions in some jurisdictions.*

- *Samples claims are found in Appendix H.*

4.4.8 PETITION

- The sample petition in Appendix A is based on an applicant who is a single inventor, not a public servant, who is a small entity, filing an application without a priority claim.

- The form of petition is prescribed in Form 1, Schedule I of the Patent Rules. (The boldface letters throughout this section refer to the sample document found in Appendix A.)

  a Fill in the full legal name of the inventor/applicant.

  b Fill in the full mailing address of the inventor/applicant. (*In some cases this may be in care of the applicant (owner).*)

- Distinguish between contributions which do not make a person an inventor and contributions which constitute inventorship. (*See section 2.7, above, for more details on this point.*)

- An inventor is a person who contributes an element to a claim. That person provides the specific creative concept which results in the particular invention described in that claim. *Note that only the inventor or legal representative may apply for a patent (section 27(1), Patent Act). Mere testing of an idea or concept, or non-inventive participation in the team which made the invention will not make one an inventor.*

- Persons may be joint inventors when their respective contributions form a claim of the invention. The *Patent Act* provides rules governing applications by joint inventors and the withdrawal or refusal of a joint inventor to participate (see section 31).

- A patent application made by joint inventors, if granted, is granted in the names of all of the applicants (section 31(5), *Patent Act*).

- *Note the existence and operation of certain special rules which determine inventorship (also see section 2.7, above).*

    c   Fill in the title of the invention. (*This may have been developed by the inventor and patent agent.*

    ° If this is a divisional application Section 2 would be filled in.

    ° If this is a priority application Section 4 would be completed.

    d   Fill in the small entity declaration.

- Section 2, Patent Rules, defines a "small entity" as either an "independent inventor" or "small business concern". A small entity is entitled to pay substantially reduced filing and other fees.

- An "independent inventor" is defined as an individual but excludes an individual who has assigned or is under a contractual or other legal obligation to assign any right in the invention to a person who is neither an individual nor a small business concern or a person who has so assigned and has knowledge of a subsequent assignment or obligation to assign to a person who is neither an individual nor a small business concern.

- A "small business concern" is defined as a person who is not an individual and whose gross annual revenue is not more than $2 million (a "business concern") but does not include a business concern that:

  ° is engaged in manufacturing and employs more than 100 persons;

  ° is engaged in other than manufacturing and employs more than 50 persons;

  ° has assigned or is under an obligation to assign any right in the invention to a person who is neither an individual nor a small business concern under the preceding definition; or

  ° has assigned or is under an obligation to assign any right in the invention to a person who qualifies as a small business concern under the preceding definition if that business has knowledge of any assignment or obligation to assign to a person who is neither an individual nor a small business concern under the preceding definition.

    e   Fill in the appointment of agent. (Typically the patent agent may have filled in this part of the petition for the client. If someone who is not a registered patent agent has assisted in the preparation of the application and no patent agent is appointed, then the applicant should notify the Patent Office of the person who so assisted.)

f Fill in the place (*i.e.*, city or town) where signed and identify the place.

g Fill in the country where signed.

h Fill in the date when signed.

i The inventor should sign in his or her normal handwriting.

• Review the form with the inventor before it is signed. *This is important since only the true inventor (or his or her successor in title) may make the application. If, for example, your client sees an invention in Europe that he or she wishes to use, the client is not the inventor and therefore cannot lawfully apply for a patent in Canada. This is the case whether or not the true inventor has applied for or obtained patent protection in Canada.*

4.4.9 REQUEST FOR EXAMINATION

• Any interested person may request examination (section 35(1), *Patent Act*).

• If examination is not requested within five years of the filing date it may be deemed abandoned (sections 35(2),73(1)(d), *Patent Act*; Rule 96.(1), Patent Rules).

• No special form is required to request an examination, however, it should be in writing and specify:

  ° the name and address of the person making the request;

  ° the name of the applicant (if the person requesting examination is not the applicant);

  ° the title of the invention;

  ° the serial number if one has been allotted to the application; and

° include the required fee (presently $200 for a small entity and $400 if not a small entity).

- In special circumstances, such as infringement or vital commercial need, you may seek expedited examination and processing of the patent application. In such a case you have to provide an affidavit setting out the basis for the request and pay the applicable fee. (See Rule 28(1), Patent Rules).

- *Note that due to treaty requirements under the PCT no patent will issue in less than 20 months.*

- *An example of a request for examination is found in Appendix B.*

4.4.10 ASSIGNMENT

- A patent application may only be filed by the inventor. In most cases the inventor will not be the owner of any rights in the invention. As a result, in such cases, a standard form assignment is filed together with or shortly after the filing of the application. In most cases this is not a negotiated agreement between the owner and the inventor. The inventor may already be obligated to assign all his or her rights to the owner. *(See section 2.7, above, on ownership.) The assignment is merely the means by which the inventor carries out his or her pre-existing obligation to the owner.*

- *An example of a standard form assignment is found in Appendix C.* The boldface letters below make reference to items in this Form. *Note that this document contains no commercial terms.*

- If the assignment is as a result of a real negotiation (*i.e.*, an acquisition of rights from the inventor after the invention has been made) then the standard form assignment might be accompanied by a separate agreement setting out the commercial terms of the assignment.

a   Fill in the full legal name of the inventor. (This should be the same spelling and wording as on the patent application.)

b   Fill in the full mailing address of the inventor.

c   Fill in the consideration paid for the assignment. (In many cases the assignment arises to perform a pre-existing legal obligation. No additional consideration is required. The form may be adapted to reflect this. More often the sum of $1 is filled in as nominal consideration. In such cases this is not a negotiation. If the assignment is as a result of a commercial negotiation the parties may not want to describe the consideration on public register. In such cases the consideration may be "pursuant to the terms of an agreement between the (Assignor) and (Assignee) and other good and valuable consideration. . . .")

d   Fill in the full legal name of the assignee.

e   Fill in the mailing address of the assignee.

f   Fill in the interest being assigned. (In most cases the assignment is an assignment of all rights in the invention.)

g   Fill in the identification of the invention assigned. (This is typically the title of the invention and serial number if one has been allotted.)

h   Fill in the place (*i.e.*, city or town) where signed and identify the place.

i   Fill in the country where signed.

j   Fill in the date when signed.

k   The inventor should sign in his or her normal handwriting.

- In some cases, the assignment must be accompanied by an affidavit of execution or other proof satisfactory to the Commissioner of Patents that the assignment has been executed by the assignor. (See section 49(3), *Patent Act.*) *In Appendix C the form for execution by an individual is shown.*

- Review the completed assignment and affidavit of execution to ensure the forms have been completely and accurately filled out and executed.

4.4.11 FILING THE APPLICATION

- The patent agent will normally file the completed application and related forms.

- In the sample case the materials forwarded to the Patent Office consist of:

  ° the patent application, including claims and drawings.

  ° duplicates.

  ° the declaration of status (if not included elsewhere).

  ° the abstract.

  ° a covering letter, which should describe the application for a patent, identify the enclosed documents, note the payment arrangements and request for stamping of the acknowledgement card and its return to you. (*See the sample letter in Appendix D.*)

  ° proper payment of the fee for the application to apply for the patent. Rule 3 of the Patent Rules requires that all remittances be made to the Commissioner of Patents. Rule 11(2) provides that payment shall be legal tender, cheques, bank drafts or money orders, and made out to the "Receiver General". (*See Appendix G for the fee schedule.*) The fees to file the application depend on whether or not the applicant is a small entity (*see section 4.4.8, above*). If the applicant is a small entity the filing fee is $150. If the applicant is not a small entity the filing fee is $300.

  ° a common practice is to add an acknowledgement card. (*See the sample in Appendix E.*) This card should be preprinted with your address and postmarked. It should identify the matter being filed and should provide a space for the Patent Office to stamp an acknowledgement of receipt of the application. The Patent Office may then mail the card back to you with evidence of the filing date. In the case of any doubt that the application was filed, the acknowledgement card is evidence of when it was filed and that it was received by the Patent Office. This may be important in some cases.

° the petition, which may include the declaration of small entity status (if applicable) and an appointment of agent.

° request for examination. Such a request need not be filed with the application. The request for examination may be combined with the covering letter sent to the Patent Office. *Note that the applicable fees for requesting examination must be added. (See Appendix G.)*

° an assignment. The assignment need not be filed with the application. Unless there is a good reason not to file the assignment it is desirable to file the assignment as early as possible to record the rights of the parties.

• Do not send models or samples unless requested to do so.

• Things to double check include:

° the spelling of all names, titles, *etc.*;

° the attachment of all attachments;

° the completeness and accuracy of the application and all forms;

° that sufficient payment has been made; and

° that you have retained copies of all documents in your file.

- Other things to do include:

  ° diarize the application. The present processing time if examination has been requested is 18 to 24 months or longer depending on the backlog at the Patent Office. If expedited review is required ensure that it has been requested and justification provided.

  ° report on the filing to your client.

  ° identify all countries your client wishes to file in.

  ° diarize the use of any treaty provision for foreign filings (*see section 3.3, above*) and address any issues surrounding filings in non-treaty countries.

4.5 CLAIMING CONVENTION PRIORITY

- Discuss claiming priority based on a foreign application with the patent agent.

- The example above is based on a Canadian inventor making application without a priority claim. An inventor may have a priority claim if he or she filed the first (priority) application in another country (*i.e.*, the United States). A foreign applicant is entitled to claim a priority based on filing a corresponding application in another country if that other country provides by convention, treaty or reciprocity the same right to Canadians. (See section 28.2(1)(d)(i)(D), *Patent Act.*)

- An application claiming priority under the Paris Convention must be filed within 12 months of the first foreign (priority) filing. (*See section 3.3, above, for more details.*)

- To claim such priority the applicant must:

  ° specifically request such treatment by the Patent Office; and

° inform the Commissioner of Patents of the filing date and application serial number in the foreign country.

- The Patent Office may require the applicant to file a certified copy of the priority application in the Canadian Patent Office. (See Rule 89, Patent Rules.)

- The Patent Office may require the applicant to file a certificate from the office in which the priority application was filed showing the actual date of filing. (See Rule 89, Patent Rules.)

- The priority claims arising from an application filed under the PCT and designating Canada are communicated by the International Bureau of the WIPO. *Section 3.3.2, above, and the PCT Applicants Guide, published by WIPO, for more details.*

5

TAKING ACTION

5.1 AN OVERVIEW OF THE PROCESS

- In Canada, it may take several years for a patent application to issue, if patentable.

- The steps in the routine prosecution of a patent application after the filing of the application include:

  ° an internal review of the application in the Patent Office;

  ° issue of a filing receipt for the patent application;

  ° filing a request for examination in the Patent Office (if not done earlier);

  ° the examiner classifies the invention and an official search is carried out;

  ° the examiner reviews the patent application against the prior art and issues an official letter (the office action);

  ° the applicant reviews and responds to the office action;

  ° if found patentable, the examiner issues a notice of allowance;

  ° the applicant must pay an issue or registration fee;

  ° the patent will issue; and

  ° throughout this process annual maintenance fees will be due.

5.2 RESPONDING TO THE PATENT OFFICE

- The staff at the Patent Office review the application for a patent. If there are errors or missing elements of the application the Patent Office will request correction or clarification.

- Personal attendance at the Patent Office is not necessary. You may communicate with the Commissioner of Patents by correspondence(Rule 5(2), Patent Rules). You may telephone the Patent Office and enquire as to the status of an application more than eight weeks after filing. *You should quote your file number.* (See Rule 7, Patent Rules.)

- You should send your client a copy of your filing receipt, and identify the filing date and serial number. You should remind your client about the deadline for any convention or treaty filings (*see section 3.3, above*).

- *Watch the time limits for responding to the Patent Office (see section 78, Patent Act).*

- The examiner will require response to the office action within the specified time period from the date of the office action. If the applicant fails to respond by that date the application may be abandoned.

- Diarize the date for a response to any official communication.

- The response should address each point or issue raised by the examiner.

- If the application is abandoned it may be possible, in certain circumstances, to seek to reinstate the application. A fee for reinstatement may be required in such circumstances. (See Rules 97, 98, Patent Rules.)

- Correspondence relating to an application may be filed by mail or delivered. It must be addressed to the Commissioner of Patents (Rule 5) and correspondence must be conducted only by the applicant or his or her patent agent (Rule 6(1)). Other requirements include:

° the serial number if one has been assigned;

° the name of the applicant or inventor;

° the title of the invention; and

° the date of allowance, if allowed (see Rule 7, *Patent Rules*).

• Correspondence directed to the Patent Office is deemed received on the date deposited in the Patent Office or an Industry Canada regional or district office (see for example Notice, p. 113 in vol. 41, No. 2066 of the *Trade Marks Journal*). (Rule 5(2), Patent Rules).

• The address of the Patent Office is:

> The Commissioner of Patents
> Industry Canada
> 50 Victoria Street
> Place du Portage, Phase I
> Hull, Quebec
> K1A 0C9
> Telephone: (819) 997-1936.

• Office hours are 8:30 am to 4:45 pm Eastern Time, Monday through Friday, except for statutory holidays.

• Other than for protests filed under section 34.1 of the *Patent Act*, a request for examination filed by a person under section 35(1) or as otherwise provided in the Act or Rules, the Patent Office will not have regard to correspondence regarding an application other than from the person with whom the Office is corresponding on the application (Rule 6(1), Patent Rules).

5.3 THE INITIAL PROCESS

- The Patent Office carries out certain internal activities with respect to a patent application.

- The application for a patent is reviewed to determine if all of the elements of the application have been properly filed and that all basic requirements have been satisfied.

- The Patent Office will issue a filing receipt indicating the filing date (which may establish your client's priority date) and a serial number to identify the application.

- *The serial number must be used to identify the application in any further communications with the Patent Office.*

5.4 THE OFFICE ACTION

- The rules governing prosecution of an application are set out in Rules 28 to 30 of the Patent Rules.

5.4.1 THE EXAMINER'S ROLE

- The stated role of the Patent Office in granting patents is to acquire and disseminate technological information and to encourage the creation, adoption and exploitation of inventions.

- The examiner classifies the invention. By identifying the classification of the invention the examiner is better able to carry out a search in the Patent Office.

- The examiner's role is to review the patent application for compliance with the requirements of the patent law, the rules and current practice.

- The examiner seeks to ensure that the applicant does not improperly obtain a patent with claims that are broader than those permitted by law.

5.4.2 THE EXAMINER'S SEARCH AND REPORT

- The examiner carries out a search of prior patents and other published documents. For example, the examiner may identify some trade or scientific journals which he or she may believe to be relevant to the subject-matter of the application.

- The examiner will examine the claims in light of the written disclosure to ensure it complies with the law and that the claims are supported by the specification. The examiner also reviews the claims in light of the prior art identified in his or her search to determine if the application describes an invention and will reject those claims which he or she believes describe matter that is old, without utility or lacks an inventive step (*i.e.*, is obvious).

- If the examiner uncovers prior art which appears to impact on the novelty or inventive merit of the application it will be cited against the specific claims in question in the office action or official letter from the examiner. If the examiner identifies any technical issues or problems with the application these will be also cited to the applicant in office action. Moreover, the examiner may reject all or some of the claims, require modification to claims to make them allowable, or allow some or all of the claims.

- Often the patent agent seeks to get the broadest possible protection which may result in some claims being too broad. In such cases it should be expected to get a rejection of such claims from the examiner.

- *Note that the office action may also require modification of the claims and sometimes drawings.*

- Copies of any prior art cited against the application will be attached to the office action.

- The examiner will require response to the office action by a specific date. If the applicant fails to respond by that date the application may be abandoned.

• The applicant responds to the office action in an amendment letter.

5.4.3 INVENTOR'S EXAMINATION OF THE CITED PRIOR ART

• The applicant should carefully review the issues raised in the office action.

• If amendments can be made without affecting the scope of protection available for the invention then they should be made.

• If amendments would affect the scope of protection available for the invention then they should be considered from the perspective of:

  ° whether the amendments might be acceptable;

  ° whether the amendments might be acceptable in certain circumstances and, if so, if those circumstances apply; or

  ° whether the applicant may be able to resist making the required amendments.

• If prior art has been cited against the invention then the prior art should be considered from the perspective of:

  ° whether the application may be amended in an acceptable form to overcome the prior art; or

  ° whether the applicant may be able to resist making any amendments, for example, by distinguishing the invention described in the application from the cited prior art.

• *Note that the deadline to respond to the office action is typically six months. Failure to respond may result in abandonment of the application. (See Rule 98, Patent Rules)*

- Diarize the date for a response to any official communication.

5.5 THE BUSINESS DECISION

- Your client has to determine whether or not to proceed with the prosecution of his or her patent application in light of the office action received.

- The client may need some assistance in evaluating the potential strength of any claims and in evaluating the likelihood of overcoming objections raised by the examiner. He or she will need some assessment of the cost and risk involved in determining how much further effort and money to dedicate to the effort.

- Decisions on foreign filings may benefit from an analysis of the likely strength of the claims which may be allowed.

- If the application has been the subject of a final rejection your client must weigh the costs and chance of success of an appeal against the importance of the registration in the client's business and marketing plans.

- You should review the strengths and weaknesses of patent protection, the risks of no protection and alternative forms of protection with your client and the patent agent to assist your client in making an informed decision.

5.6 APPEALS

- If you or the patent agent are unable to convince the examiner to accept your client's arguments in respect of an application the examiner will issue a final rejection. *At this stage, if you do not satisfy the examiner's requirements, the application will be rejected.*

- You may appeal the final rejection to the Commissioner of Patents who will set up an appeal board to hear the appeal. If you are unable to convince the Commissioner of Patents to accept your client's arguments in respect of an application the Commissioner of Patents will refuse the application (section 40, *Patent Act*).

- You may appeal the refusal to issue the patent to the Federal Court which has exclusive jurisdiction to hear such appeals (section 41, *Patent Act*).

- An appeal must be filed within six months of the final rejection (section 41, *Patent Act*).

- A further appeal from the Federal Court's decision may be attempted to the Federal Court of Appeal and subsequently the Supreme Court of Canada.

5.7 CORRECTION OF ERRORS

- The *Patent Act* and Rules provide a number of ways in which errors of various sorts may be corrected.

5.7.1 AMENDING THE APPLICATION

- Unless otherwise provided by the Patent Rules, an application may be amended by the applicant on his or her own initiative or after a request from the examiner (See Rule 31, Patent Rules for limits on the ability to amend the application).

- Amendments must be in writing and must explain the nature and purpose of the amendment (Rule 34, Patent Rules).

- Clerical errors in any instrument of record in the Patent Office do not invalidate the instrument. Such errors may be corrected under the authority of the Commissioner of Patents (section 8, *Patent Act*). For an example of correction of an error see *Bristol-Myers Squibb Co. v. Canada* (1999), 82 C.P.R. (3d) 192 (Fed. C.A.).

- You cannot add new matter and seek to back date it to the original filing date. No amendment to the disclosure is permitted if it describes matter not shown in the drawings or reasonably to be inferred from the specification as originally filed (See Section 38.2, *Patent Act*). Claims based on new matter will have a later priority date.

5.7.2 FILING A SECOND APPLICATION

- In certain circumstances your client may refile his or her application within a year of the original filing date. The replacement application may permit the applicant to correct minor errors in the first application and keep the original filing date. *You cannot add new subject-matter to the application under this procedure.*

- In order to refile, the first application must not have been refused, published, abandoned or withdrawn.

- *You cannot have used the first patent application as a priority application for foreign filings if you wish to use this procedure.*

5.7.3 AMENDMENTS AFTER ALLOWANCE

- In certain cases a notice of allowance may be withdrawn if the Commissioner of Patents finds, before issue, that the application is not allowable (Rule 30(7), Patent Rules).

- After allowance the applicant can no longer make amendments to the application (Rule 31, Patent Rules).

5.7.4 DISCLAIMERS

- If the claims are too broad-based on the prior art or specification, and if such is due to inadvertence, accident or mistake, the applicant may disclaim portions of the patent (section 48, *Patent Act*).

- The patentee would generally prefer to use this process as compared with the alternative of an adversarial review of the patent in litigation. In disclaimer proceedings the applicant does not face the arguments of the litigant.

5.7.5 REISSUE

- Reissue generally is used to expand or broaden the claims in a patent where they were erroneously defective.

- If due to insufficient description or specification a patent is considered to be defective or inoperative (*i.e.*, the patentee claimed more or less than he or she had a right to claim) then it may be possible to correct the problem by requesting reissue of the patent.

- If the problem is shown to have been caused by inadvertence, accident or mistake, and if the patent is surrendered to the Commissioner of Patents within four years of its grant, the Commissioner of Patents may cause a new patent to be issued with an amended description and specification (section 47(1), *Patent Act*; see also Rule 43, Patent Rules and section 47, *Patent Act* for procedure and rules on reissue).

- The patentee would generally prefer to use this process as compared with the alternative of an adversarial review of the patent in litigation. In reissue proceedings the applicant does not face the arguments of the other litigant.

5.7.6 REINSTATEMENT OF ABANDONED APPLICATIONS

- If a patent application is abandoned the applicant may request reinstatement and must provide proof of when the application was discovered to be abandoned and the steps taken towards reinstatement of the application. (See section 73, *Patent Act*.)

5.7.7 RE-EXAMINATION

- If a patent was not tested against certain printed publications it is possible to have the patent re-examined in light of such prior art. (*See section 3.5.5, above, for more details on re-examination.*)

5.8 ISSUE

- If the application is complete, the requirements of registration are met, and any requirements of the examiner have been satisfied, the application will normally proceed to allowance.

- Normally the grant of a patent (if the invention is patentable) will be issued within two to four years of filing the application and if examination is requested on filing. Since the Patent Office staff are often overworked the time for examination depends on the workload then pending in the Office.

- In certain exceptional cases, such as a case of infringement, it may be possible to obtain expedited examination of the Patent. (*See section 4.4.9, above, for details.*)

- At allowance the Commissioner of Patents may require the applicant to provide an abstract of the disclosure and any replacement sheets or drawings he or she may require for satisfactory reproduction by the Patent Office (Rule 34, Patent Rules).

5.9 PRESUMPTIONS ARISING FROM ISSUE

- Section 43(2) of the *Patent Act* provides that an issued patent, unless there is evidence to the contrary, shall be presumed to be valid.

- This presumption is not easy to dislodge: see *Diversified Products Corp. v. Tye-Sil Corp.* (1987), 16 C.P.R. (3d) 207

(Fed. T.D.), affirmed (1991), 35 C.P.R. (3d) 350 (Fed. C.A.);
Adamson v. Kenworthy (1931), 49 R.P.C. 57 (Eng. Ch. Div.).

- This presumption is often useful in seeking to establish the
  plaintiff's rights in an application for an interlocutory injunction.

5.10 PROTECTION IN OTHER COUNTRIES

- *In seeking to protect a work in other countries, remember that
  the Paris Convention and PCT both operate on a national
  treatment basis.*

- A Canadian patent applicant will have the same rights in a
  convention country in which he or she files an application as
  are provided by the domestic patent law of that country to
  domestic applicants.

- A Canadian patent applicant may expect certain minimum
  rights under the domestic patent law of a convention country
  as might be mandated by the General Agreement on Tariffs
  and Trade ("GATT") and the Trade Related Intellectual
  Property Standards ("TRIPS") agreement arising from the
  Uruguay round.

- A Canadian patent applicant may encounter broader (or
  narrower) protection, remedies or exemptions under the domestic patent law in a convention country.

- A patent applicant seeking international protection should
  always review the scope and extent of protection arising under the domestic law of each country of interest.

- Some countries are not members of either the Paris Convention or PCT. *See section 3.3, above, for more details.*

6

CLOSING THE FILE

6.1 DEALINGS WITH THE RIGHTS

6.1.1 ASSIGNMENTS AND LICENCES

- Patents and interests in patents are assignable (section 50, *Patent Act*, Rule 37, Patent Rules).

- Note special requirements of other legislation in some cases, such as "Every bill or note the consideration of which consists, in whole or in part, of the purchase money of a patent right, or of a partial interest, limited geographically or otherwise, in a patent right, shall have written or printed prominently and legibly across the face thereof, before it is issued, the words "Given for a patent right". Section 13(1), *Bills of Exchange Act*, R.S.C. 1985, c. B-4, as amended.

- Assignments, licences and other grants of interests should be in writing, with satisfactory proof of execution (section 50(3), *Patent Act*; Rule 37, Patent Rules) and should be recorded in the Patent Office (section 50(2), *Patent Act*).

- File the original or certified copy of the original document (Rule 37, Patent Rules).

- An assignment is void against any subsequent assignee unless the assignment has been registered in the Patent Office (section 51, *Patent Act*). Registration of an assignment or licence provides constructive notice of the registrant's claim.

- In many commercial situations the parties do not wish to record all of the terms of their agreement or licence and thereby disclose all of the commercial terms between the parties. It is not necessary to register the commercial agreement (Rule 37, Patent Rules). As a result, a short form assignment might be registered. *An example of such an assignment is attached in Appendix C.*

- *There are a number of legal advantages to registration of interests in a patent, particularly in enforcement of the patent against infringers and establishment of rights against a subsequent assignee.*

- An assignment does not by itself revoke the appointment of the patent agent (Rule 40, Patent Rules).

6.1.2 SECURITY INTERESTS

- You may register a security interest in a patent application or in a patent in the Patent Office, however there is no specific register for security interests. These are often registered as assignments.

- Consider registration of any security interest under the personal property security legislation in any applicable provinces.

- Because of possible competing interests and the doctrine of paramountcy, you should consider registration in both the federal and applicable provincial registries.

6.1.3 BANKRUPTCY

- The *Bankruptcy Act* has special provisions which apply to patented products.

- A trustee in bankruptcy has the right to sell patented articles without being bound by the restrictions or limitations which may have been imposed by the patentee (section 82(1), *Bankruptcy Act*).

- If the manufacturer or vendor of the patented products objects to sale by the trustee in bankruptcy by giving notice to the trustee, the manufacturer may purchase the articles for the invoice price thereof less reasonable deduction for depreciation (section 82(1), *Bankruptcy Act*).

- *These issues might be considered in any licence or other agreement dealing with sale of patented products.*

6.2 MARKING

- The placement of a patent notice is not mandatory but may act to give notice of the patentee's rights.

- Care should be taken to avoid misrepresentation in a patent notice as in some cases this may be an offence under section 75 or 76, *Patent Act. (See section 2.9, above, for more detail on notices.)*

6.3 MAINTENANCE FEES

- Diarize the requirement to pay maintenance fees to maintain the patent application and/or patent in force.

- Annual maintenance fees due are:

   ° if a small entity — $50 to $200*

   ° otherwise — $100 to $400*

- *See section 1.5.4, above, for further details of the requirements to pay maintenance fees. See also section 4.4.8, above, for further details on what qualifies as a small entity.*

---

* Maintenance fees increase during the term of the application/patent. For details see Appendix G.

- Failure to pay maintenance fees may prematurely end the term of the patent. (See Rule 99(1), Patent Rules, and sections 27.1, 73(1) *Patent Act*.)

6.4 INTERNATIONAL PRIORITY

- *For details on claiming convention priority for filing in Canada see Chapter 4 and section 29, Patent Act.*

- *For details and examples showing the advantages of claiming convention priority for filing see section 3.3, above.*

- Your client's ability to claim convention priority in filings in foreign countries depends on, among other factors:

  ° whether the foreign country is a member of the Paris Convention or PCT or has other bilateral or multilateral treaty arrangements with Canada;

  ° the requirements of the domestic law of the foreign country and any procedural or substantive requirements imposed (for example, provision of a certified copy of the application filed in Canada, *etc.*);

  ° the proper filing of the corresponding application within 12 months of the priority filing date (*i.e.*, the first filing date) for claim under the Paris Convention or, as applicable, having filed an application under the PCT and having designated the applicable countries (if members of the PCT) and having paid the applicable fees; or

  ° any prior publication or making available to the public of the elements of the invention.

6.5 ENFORCEMENT ACTION

- A person who infringes a patent is liable to the patentee and all persons claiming under the patentee for all damages sustained by the patentee and such persons claiming under the patentee from the infringement (section 55(1), *Patent Act*; See also section 3.5, above).

- Action against an infringer must be brought within six years of the infringing activity (section 55.01, *Patent Act*). See D. Vaver, "Limitations in Intellectual Property: 'The Time is Out of Joint' ", (1994) 73:4 Can. Bar Rev. 451 for a useful critique of limitation periods.

- An action for infringement may be brought in the Federal Court of Canada or in a provincial court with the jurisdiction necessary for the remedies sought (sections 54(1) and (2), *Patent Act*).

- Injunctive relief is available in applicable circumstances to enjoin further use, manufacture or sale of the subject-matter of a patent. Further, a court may make such order as it sees fit for and respecting inspection or account or otherwise relating to the proceedings (section 57(1), *Patent Act*).

- For more information on seeking or defending against applications for injunctive relief see Obtaining Injunctions, 1999, Carswell Practice Guide.

Appendix A

Petition

FORM 3

(Subsection 27(2) of the Patent Act)

Petition for Grant of a Patent

1. The applicant, ___**a**___, whose complete address is ___**b**___, requests the grant of a patent for an invention, entitled___**c**___, which is described and claimed in the accompanying specification.

2. This application is a division of application number _____, filed in Canada on _____ .

3. (1) The applicant is the sole inventor.

(2) The inventor is ___**a**___, whose complete address is ___**b**___, and the applicant owns in Canada the whole interest in the invention.

4. The applicant requests priority in respect of the application on the basis of the following previously regularly filed application:

Country of filing	Application number	Filing date
_____	_____	_____
_____	_____	_____

5. The applicant appoints ___**e**___, whose complete address in Canada is_____, as the applicant's representative in Canada, pursuant to section 29 of the *Patent Act*.

6. The applicant appoints ___**e**___, whose complete address is _____, as the applicant's patent agent.

7. The applicant believes that the applicant is entitled to claim status as a "small entity" as defined under section 2 of the *Patent Rules*. ___**d**___

8. The applicant requests that Figure No. _____ of the drawings accompany the abstract when it is open to public inspection under section 10 of the *Patent Act* or published.

135

Signed at _____ **f** _____ **g** _____
                     City or town   Country

this _____ **h** _____ day of _____.

_____
                                        Signature

_____
                                        Signature

Appendix B

Request For Examination

[Your name and contact address]

[Date]

The Commissioner of Patents
Industry Canada
50 Victoria Street
Place du Portage, Phase I
Hull, Quebec K1A 0C9

Attention: The Commissioner of Patents, Ottawa, Canada.

Regarding: Patent Application
                 [the title of the invention]
                 [the serial number if one has been allotted to the application]
                 Filed [filing date, if already filed]
                 Our File:

Dear Sirs;

The [the name of the applicant requesting examination (if the person requesting examination is not the applicant)] hereby requests the examination of the above mentioned patent application.

[Add the reason for making the request (if the person requesting examination is not the applicant)]

Attached hereto please find payment of the required fee and a self addressed postage prepaid acknowledgement card. Would you kindly stamp or mark the acknowledgement card with the date of receipt of this request for examination and return it to the undersigned.

[The fee for a request for examination is presently $200 for a small entity and $400 if not a small entity. (*See section 4.4.8, above, for a discussion of what constitutes a small entity.*)]

Yours truly,

Appendix C

Assignment

FORM 26

(*s. 142*)

ASSIGNMENT OF ALL INTEREST (OR AN UNDIVIDED FRACTIONAL INTEREST) IN AN INVENTION BEFORE THE ISSUE OF A PATENT

I, _____ **a** _____

whose full post office address is _____ **b** _____

in consideration of $ _____ **c** _____

the receipt of which is hereby acknowledged do hereby sell and assign to _____

_____
d
Full name of assignee

whose full post office address is _____ **e** _____

_____

all (or an undivided (state particular fractional interest) of all) my interest in Canada

in and to my invention relating to _____

f

Title of invention

as fully described and claim in my application for a patent of such invention and to all (or an undivided (state particular fractional interest) of all) my corresponding right, title and interest in and to any patent which may issue therefor.

Signed at _____ **g** _____ **h** _____
                   City or town   Country

this _____ **i** _____ day of _____.

Witness _____ **j** _____

_____
k
Signature of assignor

[The assignment must be accompanied by proof of its execution such as an affidavit of execution following Forms 27, 28 or 29, as the case may be. See sections 49(3) and 50(3), *Patent Act.*]

FORM 27

(s. 142)

AFFIDAVIT OF EXECUTION OF AN ASSIGNMENT EXECUTED BY AN INDIVIDUAL

I, _____

whose full post office address is _____
make oath and say:

That I was personally present and did see_____

_____

Name of assignor

who is personally known to me to be the person named in the attached assignment duly
sign and execute the same.

Sworn before me at

    City or town   Signature

    Country

this _____

day of _____ , _____

    Notary public

(or other official having authority to
take affidavits in the place where the
affidavits are sworn.)

Appendix D

Covering Letter to the Patent Office

[Your name and contact address]

[Date]

The Commissioner of Patents
Industry Canada
50 Victoria Street
Place du Portage, Phase I
Hull, Quebec K1A 0C9

Attention: The Commissioner of Patents, Ottawa, Canada.

Regarding: Patent Application
                    [the title of the invention]
                    [the name of the applicant]
                    Our File:

Dear Sirs;

Attached please find an application for a patent for an invention made by [the inventor] and entitled [title of invention] consisting of:

1. a petition for a patent duly executed;

2. an abstract of the invention;

3. the specification for the invention and drawings related thereto;

4. an assignment of the rights in the invention to [name of assignee];

5. the fee for the application to apply for the patent. Please note that the applicant is a small entity. [The filing fees are $150 for a small entity. If the applicant is not a small entity, the filing fee is $300. *See section 4.4.8, above, for details.*]

6. [Decide whether or not to make a request for examination and pay the examination fee at this stage; *see section 4.4.9, above.*]

7. [There is no claim of priority in this example.]

8. a self addressed postage prepaid acknowledgement card.

Would you kindly stamp or mark the acknowledgement card with the date of receipt of this request for examination and return it to the undersigned.

Yours truly,

Appendix E

Acknowledgement Card

THE PATENT OFFICE HEREBY ACKNOWLEDGES RECEIPT OF THE FOL-
LOWING:

DATED:

APPLICANT:

SERIAL NO.:

**(KINDLY APPLY
OFFICIAL RECEIPT
STAMP HERE.)**

FILE NO.:

DUE DATE:

[The reverse side of the card is self-addressed and stamped for mailing back to your office.]

Appendix F

Patent Forms

Current forms may be found at the Canadian Intellectual Property Office Website at
<http://www.patentsl.ic.gc.ca>

SCHEDULE I

(Sections 43, 44 and 77)

PRESCRIBED FORMS

FORM 1

(Section 47 of the Patent Act)

Application for Reissue

1. The patentee of Patent No. _____, granted on _____ for an invention entitled _____, requests that a new patent be issued, in accordance with the accompanying amended specification, for the unexpired term for which the original patent was granted and agrees to surrender the original patent effective on the issue of a new patent.

2. The name and complete address of the patentee is _____.

3. The respects in which the patent is deemed defective or inoperative are _____.

4. The error arose from inadvertence, accident or mistake, without any fraudulent or deceptive intention, in the following manner: _____.

5. The knowledge of the new facts giving rise to the application were obtained by the patentee on or about _____ in the following manner: _____.

6. The patentee appoints _____, whose complete address in Canada is _____, as the patentee's representative in Canada pursuant to section 29 of the *Patent Act*.

7. The patentee appoints _____, whose complete address is _____, as the patentee's patent agent.

FORM 2

(Section 48 of the Patent Act or the Act as it read immediately before October 1, 1989)

Disclaimer

1. The patentee of Patent No. _____, granted on _____ for an invention entitled _____, has, by mistake, accident or inadvertence, and without any wilful intent to defraud or mislead the public,

    (*a*)   made the specification too broad, claiming more than that of which the patentee or the person through whom the patentee claims was the (first) inventor; or

    (*b*)   in the specification, claimed that the patentee or the person through whom the patentee claims was the (first) inventor of any material or substantial part of the invention patented of which the patentee was not the (first) inventor, and to which the patentee had no lawful right.

2. The name and complete address of the patentee is _____.

3. (1) The patentee disclaims the entirety of claim _____.

(2) The patentee disclaims the entirety of claim _____ with the exception of the following: _____.

FORM 3

(Subsection 27(2) of the Patent Act)

Petition for Grant of a Patent

1. The applicant, _____, whose complete address is _____, requests the grant of a patent for an invention, entitled _____, which is described and claimed in the accompanying specification.

2. This application is a division of application number _____, filed in Canada on _____.

3. (1) The applicant is the sole inventor.

(2) The inventor is _____, whose complete address is _____, and the applicant owns in Canada the whole interest in the invention.

4. The applicant requests priority in respect of the application on the basis of the following previously regularly filed application:

Country of filing	*Application number*	*Filing date*
_____	_____	_____
_____	_____	_____

5. The applicant appoints _____, whose complete address in Canada is _____, as the applicant's representative in Canada, pursuant to section 29 of the *Patent Act*.

6. The applicant appoints _____, whose complete address is _____, as the applicant's patent agent.

7. The applicant believes that the applicant is entitled to claim status as a "small entity" as defined under section 2 of the *Patent Rules*.

8. The applicant requests that Figure No. _____ of the drawings accompany the abstract when it is open to public inspection under section 10 of the *Patent Act* or published.

FORMER FORM 24

[Example of a Patent Disclosure]

ABSTRACT

In a tool for driving posts, it is known to have a guide depending from the hammer to freely embrace the post and slide longitudinally on it. In this invention, handles are secured to the guide such that they extend lengthwise along the outside of it. The tool with the handles may have a lighter hammer and thus may be manually operated since the handles enable the operator to use his own strength to bring the hammer down on the post and hold it against rebound. The guide may have filling pieces secured to the inside to adapt its cross section to the cross section of the post being driven.

SPECIFICATION

The specification shall begin immediately following the abstract or at the top of a new page and shall consist of unnumbered paragraphs in which the following matters shall be dealt with in approximately the following order:

(1) The general character of the class of article or the kind of process to which the invention (i.e., the inventive idea) relates.

"This invention relates to a manually operable tool for driving posts into the ground."

(2) The nature in general terms of the articles or processes previously known or used which are intended to be improved or replaced by resort to the invention and of the difficulties and inconveniences which they involve.

"It is common in devices for driving piles and posts to pull up a weight or hammer, e.g., by a cable and overhead pulley arrangement, and drop it onto the end of the pile or post. It is, of course, necessary that the hammer strike the pile or post squarely, and it has been proposed to provide the hammer with a depending guide which freely embraces and may slide up and down on the post to be driven. Tools of this type are, however, inefficient because the rebound of the hammer results in a loss of energy and a tendency to split the end of the post. They are, moreover, unsatisfactory for manual operation, because the hammer must be heavy to be effective, and the power of the operator is used only in raising the heavy hammer."

(3) The inventive idea which the new article or process embodies, and the way in which resort to it overcomes the difficulties and inconveniences of previous practices or proposals.

"I have found that these disadvantages may be overcome by providing a number of handles secured to the guide and extending lengthwise along the outside of it. Such handles permit the use of a lighter hammer and the elimination of the overhead arrangement, secure a greater effect for the same amount of energy, and reduce splitting of the post, since the power of the operator of the device is used not only to raise the hammer but also to bring it down on the post and hold it against rebound."

(4) A full description of the best way of using or putting into operation the inventive idea. If there are drawings, the description should be preceded by a list of these drawings and should be related to them by the use of the numerals which appear upon them. The form of the list and of the description is illustrated by the following:

"In drawings which illustrate embodiments of the invention,

Figure 1 is an elevation partly in section of one embodiment,

Figure 2 is a top plan view of this embodiment,

Figure 3 is a section of the line III-III of Figure 1, and

Figure 4 is a plan view of another embodiment having only two handles.

The tool illustrated comprises a guide 1 which is adapted freely to embrace and slide up and down on a post A which is to be driven. It may be of any suitable cross section, but, in the form shown, is a cylinder open at the bottom and closed by a plug 2 at the top which may be the top of the device. The plug 2, which acts as a hammer, fits within the cylinder 1 and is flanged at its edge so as to lie flush with the outer wall of the cylinder. Extending lengthwise of the guide 1 are handles 3 which may be formed from metal tubes, as shown or may, if desired, be made from rods or bars covered with wood facings.

The handles 3 are secured at their upper ends to bridge pieces 4, e.g., by welding, and the bridge pieces 4 are secured as by welding to the plug 2. At their lower ends the handles 3 are flattened for engagement between two arms of a sectional clamping ring 5 fitting around the guide 1 and clamped to it by bolts 6. The lower ends of the handles are extended below the clamping ring, as indicated at 7, for the attachment of extension members (not shown) and, for this purpose, bolt holes 8 are provided in the extensions 7.

In order to adapt a guide of circular internal cross section to a square post, segmental filling pieces 9 have their flat faces facing inwards may be secured inside it, the distance between opposed flat faces being slightly greater than the thickness of the post. Two filling pieces may be used as shown in Figure 3, but four may be used if desired.

In the embodiment shown in Figure 4 there are only two lateral extending handles instead of four as in Figures 1-3, but otherwise the construction may be the same as that described above."

(5) If desired, other ways in which the inventive idea may be used or put into operation.

There should then follow an introduction to the claims in these words appearing at the top of a new page: —

148

"The embodiments of the invention in which an exclusive property or privilege is claimed are defined as follows:"

The claims should begin on the same page immediately following this introduction.

The following examples illustrate the general form which the claims should take:

(a) In the case of an apparatus—

1. A manually operable tool for driving posts into the ground, comprising a hammer, a depending guide adapted freely to embrace and slide up and down on the post to be driven, and handles extending lengthwise outside of the guide and rigidly secured thereto.

2. A tool as defined in claim 1 or claim 2, in which the guide has filling pieces secured to it in order to adapt its internal cross section to the cross section of the post to be driven into the ground.

(b) In the case of a process—

1. A process for cleaning the surface of metal, which comprises converting contaminating matter by chemical attack to a residual film which is readily removable by anodic treatment, and removing the formed film by connecting the metal as an anode in an electrolytic system.

2. A process as defined in claim 1, in which the metal to be cleaned is iron or steel and the chemical attack consists of treatment of the metal surface with a strongly oxidizing acid.

3. A process as claimed in claim 2, in which the residual film is removed in an electrolyte comprising one or more acids or salts thereof.

(c) In the case of an article—

1. An insulated electric conductor comprising a metal sheath, at least one conducting core and, between the core and the sheath, highly compacted mineral insulation constituted by a mixture of two or more pulverulent mineral insulating materials at least one of which will, on exposure to the atmosphere, cause the formation, over the exposed area, of a skin or layer which is substantially impermeable to moisture.

2. An insulated electric conductor as defined in claim 1, in which the insulating materials are calcium oxide and magnesia.

3. An insulated electric conductor as claimed in claim 2, in which the proportion of calcium oxide in the mixture is between 25 per cent and 40 per cent.

4. An insulated electric conductor as defined in claim 1, 2, or 3, in which the insulation resistance is not less than 250,000 ohms for an insulation thickness of 1.5 millimetres.

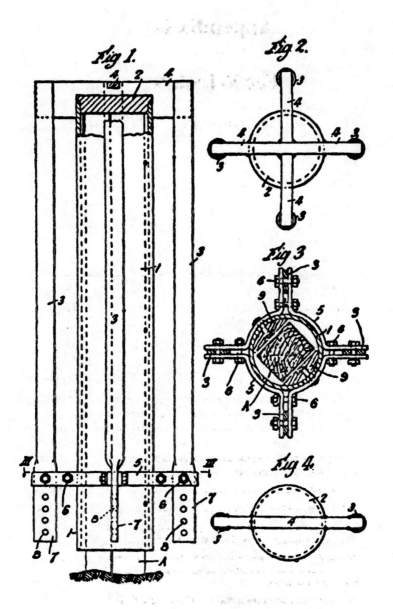

Appendix G

Fee Schedule

	Column I	Column II
Item	Description	Fee
1.	On filing an application under subsection 27(2) of the Act:	
	(*a*) small entity	$150.00
	(*b*) large entity	300.00
2.	On completing an application under subsection 94(1) or on avoiding a deemed abandonment under subsection 148(1) of these Rules:	200.00
3.	On requesting examination of an application under subsection 35(1) of the Act:	
	(*a*) small entity	200.00
	(*b*) large entity	400.00
4.	On requesting the advance of an application for examination under section 28 of these Rules	100.00
5.	On filing an amendment under subsection 32(1) of these Rules, after a notice is sent pursuant to subsection 30(1) or (5) of these Rules	200.00
6.	Final fee under subsection 30(1) or (5) of these Rules:	
	(*a*) for applications filed on or after October 1, 1989:	
	(i) basic fee	
	(A) small entity	150.00

Item	Column I Description	Column II Fee
	(B) large entity...	300.00
	(ii) plus, for each page of specification and drawings in excess of 100 pages.................................	4.00
	(b) for applications filed before October 1, 1989	
	(i) basic fee	
	(A) small entity...	350.00
	(B) large entity...	700.00
	(ii) plus, for each page of specification and drawings in excess of 100 pages.................................	4.00
7.	On requesting reinstatement of an abandoned application	200.00
8.	On applying for restoration of a forfeited application under subsection 73(2) of the Act as it read immediately before October 1, 1989......................................	200.00

PART II

INTERNATIONAL APPLICATIONS

Item	Column I Description	Column II Fee
9.	Transmittal fee under subsection 55(1) of these Rules.....	$ 200.00
10.	Basic national fee under paragraph 58(1)(c) of these Rules	
	(a) small entity	150.00
	(b) large entity	300.00
11.	Additional fee for late payment under subsection 58(3) of these Rules	200.00

PART III

PATENTS

Item	Column I Description	Column II Fee
12.	On filing an application to reissue a patent under section 47 of the Act	$ 800.00

Item	Column I Description	Column II Fee
13.	On making a disclaimer to a patent under section 48 of the Act, or of the Act as it read immediately before October 1, 1989	100.00
14.	On requesting re-examination of a claim or claims in a patent under subsection 48.1(1) of the Act:	
	(*a*) small entity	1,000.00
	(*b*) large entity	2,000.00
15.	On requesting registration of a judgment under section 62 of the Act, or of the Act as it read immediately before October 1, 1989	50.00
16.	On presenting an application to the Commissioner under subsection 65(1) of the Act:	
	(*a*) for the first patent to which the application relates	2,000.00
	(*b*) for each additional patent to which the application relates	250.00
17.	On requesting an advertisement of an application under subsection 65(1) of the Act in the *Canadian Patent Office Record* in accordance with subsection 68(2) of the Act	200.00
18.	On requesting publication in the *Canadian Patent Office Record* of a notice listing the patent numbers of patents available for licence or sale, other than at the time of issuance of the patent, for each patent number listed	20.00

PART IV

GENERAL

Item	Column I Description	Column II Fee
19.	On requesting correction of a clerical error under section 8 of the Act, or of the Act as it read immediately before October 1, 1989	$ 200.00
20.	On giving notice to the Commissioner of a new representative or a change in address, or on supplying a new and correct address, under subsection 29(3) of the Act, or of the Act as it read immediately after October 1, 1989	20.00

	Column I	Column II
Item	Description	Fee

21.	On requesting registration of a document under section 49 or 50 of the Act, or of the Act as it read immediately before October 1, 1989, or under sections 37, 38, 39 or 42 of these Rules:	
	(*a*) for the first patent or application to which the document relates	100.00
	(*b*) for each additional patent or application to which the document relates...................	50.00
22.	On applying for an extension of time under section 26 or 27 of these Rules	200.00

PART V

INFORMATION AND COPIES

	Column I	Column II
Item	Description	Fee

23.	On requesting information respecting a pending application under section 11 of the Act	$ 100.00
24.	On requesting information on whether a patent has issued, on the basis of an application filed in Canada and identified by a serial number	20.00
25.	On requesting a copy of a document, for each page	0.50
26.	On requesting a certified copy of a document	
	(*a*) for the certificate	35.00
	(*b*) for each page	0.50
27.	On requesting a copy of a Canadian patent identified by any of serial numbers 1 to 445,930.................................	4.00
28.	On requesting a copy of an audio magnetic tape..............	50.00
29.	On requesting a transcript of an audio magnetic tape, for each page in the transcript	50.00

PART VI

MAINTENANCE FEES

	Column I	Column II
Item	Description	Fee

30. For maintaining an application filed on or after October 1, 1989 in effect, under sections 99 and 154 of these Rules:

    (*a*) payment on or before the second anniversary of the filing date of the application in respect of the one-year period ending on the third anniversary:

Description	Fee
(i) small entity	$ 50.00
(ii) large entity	100.00

    (*b*) payment on or before the third anniversary of the filing date of the application in respect of the one-year period ending on the fourth anniversary:

Description	Fee
(i) small entity	50.00
(ii) large entity	100.00

    (*c*) payment on or before the fourth anniversary of the filing date of the application in respect of the one-year period ending on the fifth anniversary:

Description	Fee
(i) small entity	50.00
(ii) large entity	100.00

    (*d*) payment on or before the fifth anniversary of the filing date of the application in respect of the one-year period ending on the sixth anniversary:

Description	Fee
(i) small entity	75.00
(ii) large entity	150.00

    (*e*) payment on or before the sixth anniversary of the filing date of the application in respect of the one-year period ending on the seventh anniversary:

Description	Fee
(i) small entity	75.00
(ii) large entity	150.00

    (*f*) payment on or before the seventh anniversary of the filing date of the application in respect of the one-year period ending on the eighth anniversary:

Description	Fee
(i) small entity	75.00
(ii) large entity	150.00

    (*g*) payment on or before the eighth anniversary of the filing date of the application in respect of the one-year period ending on the ninth anniversary:

Description	Fee
(i) small entity	75.00
(ii) large entity	150.00

	Column I	Column II
Item	Description	Fee

(*h*) payment on or before the ninth anniversary of the filing date of the application in respect of the one-year period ending on the tenth anniversary:

    (i) small entity 75.00

    (ii) large entity 150.00

(*i*) payment on or before the tenth anniversary of the filing date of the application in respect of the one-year period ending on the eleventh anniversary:

    (i) small entity 100.00

    (ii) large entity 200.00

(*j*) payment on or before the eleventh anniversary of the filing date of the application in respect of the one-year period ending on the twelfth anniversary:

    (i) small entity 100.00

    (ii) large entity 200.00

(*k*) payment on or before the twelfth anniversary of the filing date of the application in respect of the one-year period ending on the thirteenth anniversary:

    (i) small entity 100.00

    (ii) large entity 200.00

(*l*) payment on or before the thirteenth anniversary of the filing date of the application in respect of the one-year period ending on the fourteenth anniversary:

    (i) small entity 100.00

    (ii) large entity 200.00

(*m*) payment on or before the fourteenth anniversary of the filing date of the application in respect of the one-year period ending on the fifteenth anniversary:

    (i) small entity 100.00

    (ii) large entity 200.00

(*n*) payment on or before the fifteenth anniversary of the filing date of the application in respect of the one-year period ending on the sixteenth anniversary:

    (i) small entity 200.00

    (ii) large entity 400.00

(*o*) payment on or before the sixteenth anniversary of the filing date of the application in respect of the one-year period ending on the seventeenth anniversary:

    (i) small entity 200.00

    (ii) large entity 400.00

	Column I	Column II
Item	Description	Fee

(*p*) payment on or before the seventeenth anniversary of the filing date of the application in respect of the one-year period ending on the eighteenth anniversary:

    (i) small entity 200.00

    (ii) large entity 400.00

(*q*) payment on or before the eighteenth anniversary of the filing date of the application in respect of the one-year period ending on the nineteenth anniversary:

    (i) small entity 200.00

    (ii) large entity 400.00

(*r*) payment on or before the nineteenth anniversary of the filing date of the application in respect of the one-year period ending on the twentieth anniversary.

    (i) small entity 200.00

    (ii) large entity 400.00

31. For maintaining the rights accorded by a patent issued on the basis of an application filed on or after October 1, 1989, under sections 100, 101, 155 and 156 of these Rules:

(*a*) in respect of the one-year period ending on the third anniversary of the filing date of the application:

    (i) fee, if payment on or before the second anniversary

        (A) small entity 50.00

        (B) large entity 100.00

    (ii) fee, including additional fee for late payment, if payment within the period of grace of one year following the second anniversary:

        (A) small entity 250.00

        (B) large entity 300.00

(*b*) in respect of the one-year period ending on the fourth anniversary of the filing date of the application:

    (i) fee, if payment on or before the third anniversary:

        (A) small entity 50.00

        (B) large entity 100.00

    (ii) fee, including additional fee for late payment, if payment within the period of grace of one year following the third anniversary:

        (A) small entity 250.00

	Column I	Column II
Item	Description	Fee

(B) large entity..	300.00
(c) in respect of the one-year period ending on the fifth anniversary of the filing date of the application:	
(i) fee, if payment on or before the fourth anniversary:	
(A) small entity..	50.00
(B) large entity..	100.00
(ii) fee, including additional fee for late payment, if payment within the period of grace of one year following the fourth anniversary:	
(A) small entity..	250.00
(B) large entity..	300.00
(d) in respect of the one-year period ending on the sixth anniversary of the filing date of the application:	
(i) fee, if payment on or before the fifth anniversary:	
(A) small entity..	75.00
(B) large entity..	150.00
(ii) fee, including additional fee for late payment, if payment within the period of grace of one year following the fifth anniversary:	
(A) small entity..	275.00
(B) large entity..	350.00
(e) in respect of the one-year period ending on the seventh anniversary of the filing date of the application:	
(i) fee, if payment on or before the sixth anniversary:	
(A) small entity..	75.00
(B) large entity..	150.00
(ii) fee, including additional fee for late payment, if payment within the period of grace of one year following the sixth anniversary:	
(A) small entity..	275.00
(B) large entity..	350.00
(f) in respect of the one-year period ending on the eighth anniversary of the filing date of the application:	
(i) fee, if payment on or before the seventh anniversary:	
(A) small entity..	75.00

	Column I	Column II
Item	Description	Fee

	(B) large entity...	150.00
	(ii) fee, including additional fee for late payment, if payment within the period of grace of one year following the seventh anniversary:	
	(A) small entity...	275.00
	(B) large entity...	350.00
	(g) in respect of the one-year period ending on the ninth anniversary of the filing date of the application:	
	(i) fee, if payment on or before the eighth anniversary:	
	(A) small entity...	75.00
	(B) large entity...	150.00
	(ii) fee, including additional fee for late payment, if payment within the period of grace of one year following the eighth anniversary:	
	(A) small entity...	275.00
	(B) large entity...	350.00
	(h) in respect of the one-year period ending on the tenth anniversary of the filing date of the application:	
	(i) fee, if payment on or before the ninth anniversary:	
	(A) small entity...	75.00
	(B) large entity...	150.00
	(ii) fee, including additional fee for late payment, if payment within the period of grace of one year following the ninth anniversary:	
	(A) small entity...	275.00
	(B) large entity...	350.00
	(i) in respect of the one-year period ending on the eleventh anniversary of the filing date of the application:	
	(i) fee, if payment on or before the tenth anniversary:	
	(A) small entity...	100.00
	(B) large entity...	200.00
	(ii) fee, including additional fee for late payment, if payment within the period of grace of one year following the tenth anniversary:	
	(A) small entity...	300.00
	(B) large entity...	400.00

Item	Column I Description	Column II Fee
	(*j*) in respect of the one-year period ending on the twelfth anniversary of the filing date of the application:	
	(i) fee, if payment on or before the eleventh anniversary:	
	(A) small entity...	100.00
	(B) large entity...	200.00
	(ii) fee, including additional fee for late payment, if payment within the period of grace of one year following the eleventh anniversary:	
	(A) small entity...	300.00
	(B) large entity...	400.00
	(*k*) in respect of the one-year period ending on the thirteenth anniversary of the filing date of the application:	
	(i) fee, if payment on or before the twelfth anniversary:	
	(A) small entity...	100.00
	(B) large entity...	200.00
	(ii) fee, including additional fee for late payment, if payment within the period of grace of one year following the twelfth anniversary:	
	(A) small entity...	300.00
	(B) large entity...	400.00
	(*l*) in respect of the one-year period ending on the fourteenth anniversary of the filing date of the application:	
	(i) fee, if payment on or before the thirteenth anniversary:	
	(A) small entity...	100.00
	(B) large entity...	200.00
	(ii) fee, including additional fee for late payment, if payment within the period of grace of one year following the thirteenth anniversary:	
	(A) small entity...	300.00
	(B) large entity...	400.00
	(*m*) in respect of the one-year period ending on the fifteenth anniversary of the filing date of the application:	
	(i) fee, if payment on or before the fourteenth anniversary:	
	(A) small entity...	100.00

	Column I	Column II
Item	Description	Fee

(B) large entity..	200.00
(ii) fee, including additional fee for late payment, if payment within the period of grace of one year following the fourteenth anniversary:	
(A) small entity..	300.00
(B) large entity...	400.00
(*n*) in respect of the one-year period ending on the sixteenth anniversary of the filing date of the application:	
(i) fee, if payment on or before the fifteenth anniversary:	
(A) small entity..	200.00
(B) large entity...	400.00
(ii) fee, including additional fee for late payment, if payment within the period of grace of one year following the fifteenth anniversary:	
(A) small entity..	400.00
(B) large entity...	600.00
(*o*) in respect of the one-year period ending on the seventeenth anniversary of the filing date of the application:	
(i) fee, if payment on or before the sixteenth anniversary:	
(A) small entity..	200.00
(B) large entity...	400.00
(ii) fee, including additional fee for late payment, if payment within the period of grace of one year following the sixteenth anniversary:	
(A) small entity..	400.00
(B) large entity...	600.00
(*p*) in respect of the one-year period ending on the eighteenth anniversary of the filing date of the application:	
(i) fee, if payment on or before the seventeenth anniversary:	
(A) small entity..	200.00
(B) large entity...	400.00
(ii) fee, including additional fee for late payment, if payment within the period of grace of one year following the seventeenth anniversary:	
(A) small entity..	400.00

	Column I	Column II
Item	Description	Fee

(B) large entity..	600.00

(*q*) in respect of the one-year period ending on the nineteenth anniversary of the filing date of the application:

(i) fee, if payment on or before the eighteenth anniversary:

(A) small entity..	200.00
(B) large entity..	400.00

(ii) fee, including additional fee for late payment, if payment within the period of grace of one year following the eighteenth anniversary:

(A) small entity..	400.00
(B) large entity..	600.00

(*r*) in respect of the one-year period ending on the twentieth anniversary of the filing date of the application:

(i) fee, if payment on or before the nineteenth anniversary:

(A) small entity..	200.00
(B) large entity..	400.00

(ii) fee, including additional fee for late payment, if payment within the period of grace of one year following the nineteenth anniversary:

(A) small entity..	400.00
(B) large entity..	600.00

32.   For maintaining the rights accorded by a patent issued on or after October 1, 1989 on the basis of an application filed before that date, under subsections 182(1) and (3) of these Rules:

(*a*) in respect of the one-year period ending on the third anniversary of the date on which the patent was issued:

(i) fee, if payment on or before the second anniversary:

(A) small entity..	$ 50.00
(B) large entity..	100.00

(ii) fee, including additional fee for late payment, if payment within the period of grace of one year following the second anniversary:

(A) small entity..	250.00
(B) large entity..	300.00

	Column I	Column II
Item	Description	Fee

(*b*) in respect of the one-year period ending on the fourth anniversary of the date on which the patent was issued:

(i) fee, if payment on or before the third anniversary:

    (A) small entity 50.00

    (B) large entity 100.00

(ii) fee, including additional fee for late payment, if payment within the period of grace of one year following the third anniversary:

    (A) small entity 250.00

    (B) large entity 300.00

(*c*) in respect of the one-year period ending on the fifth anniversary of the date on which the patent was issued:

(i) fee, if payment on or before the fourth anniversary:

    (A) small entity 50.00

    (B) large entity 100.00

(ii) fee, including additional fee for late payment, if payment within the period of grace of one year following the fourth anniversary:

    (A) small entity 250.00

    (B) large entity 300.00

(*d*) in respect of the one-year period ending on the sixth anniversary of the date on which the patent was issued:

(i) fee, if payment on or before the fifth anniversary:

    (A) small entity 75.00

    (B) large entity 150.00

(ii) fee, including additional fee for late payment, if payment within the period of grace of one year following the fifth anniversary:

    (A) small entity 275.00

    (B) large entity 350.00

(*e*) in respect of the one-year period ending on the seventh anniversary of the date on which the patent was issued:

(i) fee, if payment on or before the sixth anniversary:

    (A) small entity 75.00

	Column I	Column II
Item	Description	Fee

(B) large entity...	150.00
(ii) fee, including additional fee for late payment, if payment within the period of grace of one year following the sixth anniversary:	
(A) small entity...	275.00
(B) large entity...	350.00
(f) in respect of the one-year period ending on the eighth anniversary of the date on which the patent was issued:	
(i) fee, if payment on or before the seventh anniversary:	
(A) small entity...	75.00
(B) large entity...	150.00
(ii) fee, including additional fee for late payment, if payment within the period of grace of one year following the seventh anniversary:	
(A) small entity...	275.00
(B) large entity...	350.00
(g) in respect of the one-year period ending on the ninth anniversary of the date on which the patent was issued:	
(i) fee, if payment on or before the eighth anniversary:	
(A) small entity...	75.00
(B) large entity...	150.00
(ii) fee, including additional fee for late payment, if payment within the period of grace of one year following the eighth anniversary:	
(A) small entity...	275.00
(B) large entity...	350.00
(h) in respect of the one-year period ending on the tenth anniversary of the date on which the patent was issued:	
(i) fee, if payment on or before the ninth anniversary:	
(A) small entity...	75.00
(B) large entity...	150.00
(ii) fee, including additional fee for late payment, if payment within the period of grace of one year following the ninth anniversary:	
(A) small entity...	275.00

	Column I	Column II
Item	Description	Fee

(B) large entity..	350.00

(*i*) in respect of the one-year period ending on the eleventh anniversary of the date on which the patent was issued:

(i) fee, if payment on or before the tenth anniversary:

(A) small entity...	100.00
(B) large entity..	200.00

(ii) fee, including additional fee for late payment, if payment within the period of grace of one year following the tenth anniversary:

(A) small entity...	300.00
(B) large entity..	400.00

(*j*) in respect of the one-year period ending on the twelfth anniversary of the date on which the patent was issued:

(i) fee, if payment on or before the eleventh anniversary:

(A) small entity...	100.00
(B) large entity..	200.00

(ii) fee, including additional fee for late payment, if payment within the period of grace of one year following the eleventh anniversary:

(A) small entity...	300.00
(B) large entity..	400.00

(*k*) in respect of the one-year period ending on the thirteenth anniversary of the date on which the patent was issued:

(i) fee, if payment on or before the twelfth anniversary:

(A) small entity...	100.00
(B) large entity..	200.00

(ii) fee, including additional fee for late payment, if payment within the period of grace of one year following the twelfth anniversary:

(A) small entity...	300.00
(B) large entity..	400.00

(*l*) in respect of the one-year period ending on the fourteenth anniversary of the date on which the patent was issued:

	Column I	Column II
Item	Description	Fee

(i) fee, if payment on or before the thirteenth anniversary:

    (A) small entity 100.00

    (B) large entity 200.00

(ii) fee, including additional fee for late payment, if payment within the period of grace of one year following the thirteenth anniversary:

    (A) small entity 300.00

    (B) large entity 400.00

(*m*) in respect of the one-year period ending on the fifteenth anniversary of the date on which the patent was issued:

(i) fee, if payment on or before the fourteenth anniversary:

    (A) small entity 100.00

    (B) large entity 200.00

(ii) fee, including additional fee for late payment, if payment within the period of grace of one year following the fourteenth anniversary:

    (A) small entity 300.00

    (B) large entity 400.00

(*n*) in respect of the one-year period ending on the sixteenth anniversary of the date on which the patent was issued:

(i) fee, if payment on or before the fifteenth anniversary:

    (A) small entity 200.00

    (B) large entity 400.00

(ii) fee, including additional fee for late payment, if payment within the period of grace of one year following the fifteenth anniversary:

    (A) small entity 400.00

    (B) large entity 600.00

(*o*) in respect of the one-year period ending on the seventeenth anniversary of the date on which the patent was issued:

(i) fee, if payment on or before the sixteenth anniversary:

    (A) small entity 200.00

    (B) large entity 400.00

166

	Column I	Column II
Item	Description	Fee

	(ii) fee, including additional fee for late payment, if payment within the period of grace of one year following the sixteenth anniversary:	
	(A) small entity	400.00
	(B) large entity	600.00

PART VII

PATENT AGENTS

	Column I	Column II
Item	Description	Fee

33.	On applying for entry on the register of patent agents under section 15 of these Rules	$ 100.00
34.	On notifying the Commissioner pursuant to subsection 14(2) of these Rules of a proposal to sit for the whole or any part of the qualifying examination	200.00
35.	For maintaining the name of a patent agent on the register of patent agents pursuant to paragraph 16(1)(a) of these Rules	300.00
36.	On applying to the Commissioner for reinstatement on the register of patent agents under section 17 of these Rules	200.00

Appendix H

Sample Patent

- Attached is an issued patent Canadian Patent Number 2,042,391 filed August 21, 1990, laid open to the public on March 3, 1991 and issued January 11, 1994. Note that this application was based on the priority of a U.S. application serial number 412,344 filed September 26, 1989.

- This particular example shows an improved "Dual Writing Element Retractable Pen" invented by Mr. Roland Longarzo. The patent is reproduced with the consent of the applicant and Smart & Biggar, the patent agents for the applicant.

- This sample is intended to provide an example of how an invention may be described and how the claims might be structured. Of course you and your patent agent will need to formulate the specification including drawings and description for your client's invention(s).

Consommation et
Affaires commerciales Canada

Consumer and
Corporate Affairs Canada

Bureau des brevets

Patent Office

Ottawa, Canada
K1A 0C9

(11) (C) **2,042,391**

(88) 1990/08/21

(43) 1991/03/27

(45) 1994/01/11

(51) INTL.CL. B43K-027/08

(19) (CA) **CANADIAN PATENT** (12)

(54) Dual Writing Element Retractable Pen

(72) Longarzo, Roland , U.S.A.

(73) 2C Co. Corp. , U.S.A.

(30) (US) U.S.A. 412,344 1989/09/26

(57) 27 Claims

Canadä

CCA 3F4 (10-85) 41 7520-71-035-3354

BACKGROUND OF THE INVENTION

The present invention relates generally to improvements in writing instruments and it relates particularly to an improved multiple element writing instrument in which the writing elements may be selectively advanced to a writing position.

Protract retract dual writing element pens of the twist type are well known and widely employed. Such pens conventionally include a pair of manually accessible control components, one being a cylindrical cam and the other a longitudinal guide member and writing element engaging chucks which are restricted to longitudinal movement by the guide member having followers engaging the cam to effect such longitudinal movement of the chucks of writing elements with the relative rotation or twisting of the control components which alternatively effects the advance of a selected one of the writing elements and the withdrawal of the other.

The aforesaid twist type dual writing element is highly convenient to use but is generally complicated and expensive, requiring a large number of separate parts many of which are costly and a time consuming and laborious assembly calling for highly skilled labor. The conventional and known twist type dual element retractable pen is by reason of its complexity and cost unsuitable for use as a disposable or throw-away article.

SUMMARY OF THE INVENTION

A principal object of the present invention is the provision of an improved writing instrument.

Another object of the present invention is the provision of an improved retractable pen.

Still another object of the present invention is to provide an improved twist type retractable pen.

A further object of the present invention is to provide an improved multiple element twist type retractable pen in which the individual writing elements are selectively protractable.

Still a further object of the present invention is to provide an improved multiple writing element retractable pen comprising a minimum of components which are easily and rapidly assembled with little skill and each of which is easily moldable of a thermoplastic polymeric material to provide a rugged, reliable, and inexpensive device of attractive appearance and cheap enough to be disposable or a throw-away or giveaway.

The above and other objects of the present invention will become apparent from a reading of the following description taken in conjunction with the accompanying drawings which illustrate preferred embodiments thereof.

A retractable multiple writing element pen in accordance with the present invention includes axially coupled upper and lower barrel members, the upper barrel member having integrally formed on its inside face a first cylindrical cam portion having along its bottom a peripherally longitudinally inclined top cam surface. A second cam portion has a top face defining a bottom cam surface complementing, parallel to and spaced from the top cam surface to delineate a cylindrical cam track or groove including oppositely axially peripherally inclined cam groove sections. The second cam portion telescopes the upper barrel section with an interference fit and a mating longitudinal ridge and groove are formed in the confronting faces of the second cam and upper barrel member to precisely index and orient the top and bottom cam surfaces. A guide member having opposite longitudinal channels is rotatably axially positioned in the barrels and a writing element engaging chuck slidably engages each longitudinal channel and includes a transverse follower slidably engaging the cam groove. A writing element engages each of the chucks and extends toward the apertured tapered tip of the lower barrel member.

In one preferred embodiment of the improved pen, the guide member rotatably engages an axial bore in the upper part of the upper barrel member and extends into and is coupled to the lower barrel member to be rotatable therewith so that relative twisting of the upper and lower barrel members effects the advance and withdrawal of respective writing elements. In another preferred embodiment of the present invention, the lower cam section is integrally formed as a unit with the lower barrel member and the guide member terminates at its top in an enlarged head or knob to facilitate the manual turning of the guide member relative to the barrel to effect the writing element advance and withdrawal movements.

The improved multiple element retractable pen, in addition to the writing elements, per se, includes only five or six individual parts, each of which is molded as a single unit, of a thermoplastic or thermosetting organic polymeric resin composition, the component parts are easily and rapidly assembled, the parts interfitting and indexing formations being integrally formed on the respective components. Moreover, springs and other elements are obviated. The resulting writing instrument is rugged, reliable, simple, easily decorated and of attractive appearance and of low final cost permitting its use as a disposable giveaway and throwaway article.

BRIEF DESCRIPTION OF THE DRAWINGS

Figure 1 is an exploded perspective view of a preferred embodiment of the present invention;

Figure 2 is a longitudinal sectional view of the assembled writing instrument shown in Figure 1 with the writing elements in retracted position;

Figure 3 is a sectional view taken along line 3-3 in Figure 2 but with one writing element shown retracted and the other protracted;

Figure 4 is a sectional view taken along line 4-4 in Figure 2;

Figure 5 is a sectional view taken along line 5-5 in Figure 3;

Figure 6 is a sectional view taken along line 6-6 in Figure 3;

Figure 7 is an exploded perspective view of another preferred embodiment of the present invention;

Figure 8 is a medial longitudinal sectional view of the assembled pen of the embodiment of Figure 7 with the writing elements in retracted positions;

Figure 9 is a sectional view taken along line 9-9 in Figure 8; and

Figure 10 is a sectional view taken along line 10-10 in Figure 8.

DESCRIPTION OF THE PREFERRED EMBODIMENTS

Referring to the drawings, particularly Figures 1 to 7 thereof which illustrate a preferred embodiment of the present invention, the reference numeral 10 generally designates the improved pen which is shown as a twist type retractable dual writing element instrument. The pen 10, in addition to a pair of different writing elements 11 of conventional construction which may be different colored ink ball or other point cartridges, a lower barrel member 12, an upper barrel member 13, a lower cylindrical cam second part or section 14, a longitudinal guide member 16 and a pair of similar chuck members 17. Each of the components 12-17 is an integrally formed unit molded of a synthetic organic polymeric resin of any suitable composition which may be thermoplastic or thermosetting.

The lower barrel member 12 is mostly of tubular cylindrical shape open at its top and tapering at its bottom portion to a writing element circular bottom access opening 24. Formed on the inside face 20 of barrel member 12 is an indexing formation or ridge 18 which extends longitudinally from proximate the top of barrel member 12 to a point shortly above the tapered bottom portion of barrel member 12. Formed on the upper outside face of barrel member 12 a short distance below its top opening 20 is a collar 21 having a horizontal flat shoulder defining top face 22 and a downwardly inwardly tapering peripheral face 23.

The upper barrel member 13, in accordance with the present invention, has integrally formed therewith on its upper inside face the upper section of first part 26 of a cylindrical cam. Upper barrel member 13 is of tubular configuration with an inside diameter approximately equal to the outside diameter of collar shoulder 22 and having a circular bottom opening 27 of diameter about equal to that of shoulder 22. Cam upper section 26 has an axial bore 28 and a downwardly facing top cam face or cam surface defining bottom face 29. Cam surface 29 is substantially planar and includes 180 degree oppositely inclined cam surface sections 32 and 33, cam surface section 32 being axially counterclockwise downwardly inclined and section 33 being axially clockwise downwardly inclined; the cam surface section each extending peripherally approximately 180 degrees. Barrel member 33 terminates at its top in a flat transverse annular end face 34.

Formed on the lower inside face of upper barrel member 13 and extending from the lower edge thereof to a level below the cam surface 29 is a longitudinally extending indexing formation or ridge 36.

The lower cylindrical cam section 14 is of circular cylindrical tubular shape with an outside diameter slightly greater than the inside diameter of the lower portion of upper barrel member 13. A longitudinal indexing formation or groove 37 matching in dimensions and position the rectangular indexing ridge 36 is formed in the outside peripheral face of cam section 14. The bottom end face 38 of cam section 14 is planar and horizontal and the top end face 39 thereof which defines a bottom cam face and is flat and inclined at the angle of the bottom end face 29 of upper cam section 26 to provide a pair of oppositely inclined cylindrical cam faces 40 and 41 corresponding to cam surfaces 32 and 33. The tops and bottoms respectively of cam surfaces 40 and 41 terminate in radial triangular top and bottom vertical notches 42 and 43.

Cam section 14 telescopes and is contiguous to the enlarged lower portion of barrel member 13 with an interference or force fit, the indexing ridge 36, engaging indexing groove 37 and cam section and face 38 being coplanar with the bottom and face 44 of barrel section 33. As angularly indexed by ridge 36 and groove 37 and relatively positioned by end faces 38 and 34 cam surfaces 40 and 41 are in vertically spaced registry with and equally spaced from and parallel to cam surfaces 32 and 33, the cam surfaces delineating a cylindrical cam track or groove of uniform height including opposite oppositely inclined 180-degree cam groove sections. It should be noted that the inclined cam groove sections may be less than 180 degrees each.

The guide member 16 includes an elongated circular cylindrical rod 46 terminating at its top in an enlarged frusto-conical head 47 with a flat annular underface, the peripheral face of rod 46 shortly below head 47 having axially spaced longitudinal annular ridges

48. Formed in opposite sides of the peripheral face of rod 46 are 180-degree spaced guide channels or tracks 49 of square transverse cross section extending from shortly below ridges 48 to the bottom end of rod 46. Also formed in the outside face of rod 46 is a longitudinally extending groove 50 extending upwardly from the bottom of rod 46 and located between channels 49 and mating ridge 18 on the inside face of barrel member 12. In the assembled condition of pen 10, rod 46 rotatably engages bore 28 in barrel member 13 and the axial bore in cam section 14 and tightly engages the bore in barrel member 12 with ridge 18 engaging groove 50 so that barrel member 12 and guide member 16 rotate in unison. The underface of head 47 engages end face 34.

Each chuck member 17 includes an elongated bar 52 slidably engaging and nesting in a respective guide channel 49. The bar 52 terminates at its top in an integrally formed transversely projecting follower 53 of hexagonal transverse cross section with a lowermost angle, each follower 53 slidably engaging a respective cam groove section delineated by cam surfaces 32, 33, 40 and 41 at 180 degree spaced points. A cylindrical coupling socket 54 is formed in the lower end of each bar 52.

A pen or other writing element 11 of known construction includes a tabular reservoir 56 and terminates at its bottom in a writing tip 57. The upper end of each writing element tightly fits in a respective chuck socket 54 so that the writing elements are movable with the chuck members.

In assembling the pen 10, guide member rod 46 is inserted through upper barrel bore 28 to bring head 47 to bear on barrel end face 34. The writing element carrying chuck bars are then slid along respective guide channels 49 to bring followers 53 into engagement with upper cam surfaces 32 and 33 and thereafter cam member 40 is telescoped into barrel member 13 as angularly positioned by engaging indexing ridge 36 and groove 37. Cam member 14 is force raised in barrel member 13 by a suitable die until the bottom face of cam member 14 is coplanar with the bottom edge of barrel member 13 in which position the cam surfaces delineate a suitably wide cam channel. The upper portion of the bottom barrel member is then inserted into the bore of cam member 14 until shoulder 22 engages the bottom thereof, the lower part of guide member rod 46 telescoping the upper part of barrel member 12 with ridge 18 engaging guide member channel 50 so that the guide and lower barrel members rotate in unison. The pen and writing elements are so dimensioned that when the followers 53 engage midpoints on the respective cam channel sections both elements 11 are withdrawn into barrel 12 as shown in Figure 2, and when one follower 53 engages the upper end, the other follower 53 simultaneously engages the lower end of the corresponding cam channel section so that one writing element is fully retracted and the other writing element is fully protracted as shown in Figure 3.

In the operation of pen 10 by relatively twisting upper and lower barrel members 12 and 13, the guide member 16 angularly shifts chucks 17 which are longitudinally shifted in opposite directions by the interaction of followers 53 and the respective cam channel sections. Thus, relatively twisting the barrel members in one direction withdraws a first of the writing elements and advances the other writing element to its protracted writing position and twisting the barrel members in an opposite direction advances the first writing element to writing position and withdraws the other. Twisting the barrel members to an intermediate angular position brings both writing elements into a withdrawn position within the lower barrel member.

The embodiment of the present invention illustrated in Figures 7 to 10 of the drawings differs from that first described primarily in that the lower cam member and lower barrel section are integrally formed as a unit and the guide member is rotatable relative to the upper and lower barrel members thereby reducing the number of individually molded components.

Specifically, the improved modified pen is designated by the reference numeral 46 and includes, in addition to the ball point pen cartridges 59, a lower barrel and cam section unit 60, a pair of chuck members 61, an upper barrel and cam section member 67 and a guide member 64.

Upper barrel member 63 is of cylindrical tubular configuration including a main body portion 55 and an upper coaxial tubular stub portion 65 separated from main portion 55 by flat annular shoulder 66. Integrally formed on the inside face of body portion 55 is an upper cam section 67 similar in shape to cam section 26 of the first embodiment, cam section 67 and stub 65 having a common axial bore 68. A short longitudinal indexing ridge member 75 is formed on the lower inside face of main portion 55.

The lower barrel and cam section 60 corresponds in shape to the assembled lower barrel member 12 and cam member 14 of the first described embodiment but integrally molded as a single unit. Lower barrel member 60 includes a bottom lower barrel section 68 similar to that of barrel member 12 and an upper portion 69 defining a lower cylindrical cam section corresponding to cam section 40 and having an inclined top cam face 70 corresponding to cam face 40. It should be noted that the integral longitudinal ridge 18 in barrel member 12 is here obviated. Formed on the outside peripheral face of cam section 69 is a longitudinal indexing groove 45.

The guide member 64 includes an elongated cylindrical rod 71 having formed in opposite sides thereof track defining channels 72 of rectangular transverse cross section and extending from the bottom of rod 71 to a level a little short of the top thereof. Formed atop the rod 71 is a cup shaped coaxial cylindrical knob 73 having a hemispherical top wall 74, the inside peripheral face of knob 73 being radially spaced from the peripheral face of rod 71 to define an annular recess 76. In the assembled condition of guide member 64 and upper barrel member 63, the upper part of rod 71 rotatably engages bore 68 and stub 65 rotatably nests in annular recess 76, mating peripheral ridges and grooves' being formed in the confronting engaging faces of stub 65 and the upper part of rod 71 to prevent any axial relative movement while permitting the rotation of guide member 64.

Each chuck member 61 includes a bar of rectangular transverse cross section and slidably engages a respective guide channel 72. The guide bars 78 terminate at their top in an outwardly transversely projecting follower 79 of hexagonal transverse cross section. A coupling pin 80 axially depends from each bar 78 and each has formed on its outer face a pair of opposite detents 81. Pins 80 project into the open top ends of respective tubular writing elements 59 and are retained thereon by detents 81.

In assembling pen 58, guide bar 71 is advanced downwardly through bore 68 to bring stub 65 into engagement with annular recess 76 and locked therein against axial movement, the underface of knob 73 bearing on shoulder 66. A writing element coupled chuck member 61 is brought into sliding engagement with each guide channel 72 and raised to bring the follower 79 thereon into engagement with the bottom cam face of upper cam section 67. The lower cam section 69 is advanced upwardly in telescoping engagement with the lower inside face of cam section 63 and with indexing groove 45 and ridge 75 in sliding engagement. The lower barrel member 60 is then raised until the lower outer peripheral edge of cam section 69 is at the level of the bottom edge of upper barrel member 63 in which position the cam faces of the upper and lower cam sections delineate a cylindrical cam channel with opposite differently inclined sections which are slidably engaged by respective followers 79. The confronting peripheral faces of the upper and

175

lower cam sections are in relative movement preventing fit, for example an interference or force fit.

The operation of the pen last described is similar to that first described.

While there have been described and illustrated preferred embodiments of the present invention, it is apparent that numerous alterations, omissions and additions may be made without departing from the spirit thereof.

CLAIMS

1. A writing instrument comprising:

an upper barrel member having integrally formed on its upper inside face a cylindrical cam first part having along its bottom a top cam face;

a separate cylindrical cam second part telescoping and contiguous to the lower part of said upper barrel member and having along its top a bottom cam face complementing said top cam face and positioned and oriented relative to said top cam face to delineate a cylindrical cam track including peripherally spaced oppositely longitudinally peripherally inclined cam track sections, said upper barrel member and said cylindrical cam second part having confronting peripheral faces in mutual interference engagement;

a longitudinal guide member coaxial with and rotatable relative to said cam track and including a pair of peripherally spaced longitudinal guide tracks;

a chuck member slidably engaging each of said guide tracks and including a follower projecting transversely into sliding engagement with a respective cam track section;

a lower barrel member depending from and coaxial with said upper barrel member and terminating at its bottom end in an axial aperture; and

a writing element engaging and movable with each of said chucks and extending downwardly toward said lower barrel member bottom end.

2. The writing instrument of claim 1 wherein said guide member is coupled to and rotatable with said lower barrel member.

3. The writing instrument of claim 1 wherein said cylindrical cam second part is integrally formed with said lower barrel member as a unitary member.

4. The writing instrument of claim 3 wherein said upper barrel member has an axial bore formed in its upper part and said guide member includes a cylindrical rod rotatably engaging said upper barrel member bore and terminating at its top in a control knob.

5. The writing instrument of claim 4 wherein said upper barrel member has an upwardly projecting sleeve coaxially formed at its top and said knob has a coaxial open bottom annular socket formed in its underface rotatably engaging said sleeve.

6. The writing instrument of claim 1 wherein said guide tracks are defined by channels of rectangular transverse cross section and each of said chuck members includes a rectangular bar slideably engaging a respective guide channel.

7. The writing instrument of claim 1 wherein each of said cam track sections extends for approximately 180 degrees.

8. The writing instrument of claim 8 wherein the lower ends of the bottom faces of said cam track sections are joined by a vertical notch.

9. A dual selectively protractable writing element writing instrument comprising:

a tubular first barrel member;

a cylindrical cam coaxially locate in said barrel member and having a cylindrical cam groove with opposite oppositely inclined cam groove sections, defined by parallel axially opposite faces;

176

a longitudinally stationary rotatable guide member coaxial with said cylindrical cam and having formed therein a pair of peripherally opposite longitudinally extending guideways;

a chuck member slidably engaging each of said guideways and including a transversely projection follower slideably engaging a respective cam groove section; and

a writing element coupled to each of said chucks; said writing instrument being characterized by said cylindrical cam including axially spaced coaxial first and second cam parts with said cam groove faces being defined by the confronting spaced end faces of said cam parts, said first cam part being integrally formed with said barrel member and said second cam part telescoping and being contiguous to said first barrel member, said second cam part and said barrel member having confronting peripheral faces in mutual interference engagement.

10. The writing instrument of claim 11 including a second barrel member coaxial with said first barrel member and integrally formed as a unit with said second cam part.

11. The writing instrument of claim 12 wherein said guide member projects axially through and is rotatable relative to said first barrel member and terminates in a knob located at the outer end of said first barrel member.

12. The writing instrument of claim 10, including a second barrel member coaxial with said first barrel member and coupled to said guide member for rotation therewith.

13. The writing instrument of claim 17 wherein said upper barrel member and said cylindrical cam second part have confronting peripheral faces in mutual interference engagement.

14. The writing instrument of claim 18 wherein said second cam part and said barrel member have confronting peripheral faces in mutual interference engagement.

15. A writing instrument comprising;

an upper barrel member having integrally formed on its upper inside face a cylindrical cam first part having along its bottom a top cam face;

a cylindrical cam second part telescoping the lower part of said barrel member and having along its top a bottom cam face complementing said top cam face and positioned and oriented relative to said top cam face to delineate a cylindrical cam track including a peripherally spaced oppositely longitudinally peripherally inclined cam track sections, the confronting telescoping faces of said upper barrel member and cam second part having mating indexing formations positioning said upper barrel member and said second cam part in a predetermined relative angular relationship wherein said upper and lower cam faces are parallel and equidistant;

a longitudinal guide member coaxial with and rotatable relative to said cam track and including a pair of peripherally spaced longitudinal guide tracks;

a chuck member slidably engaging each of said guide tracks and including a follower projecting transversely into sliding engagement with a respective cam track section;

a lower barrel member depending from and coaxial with said upper barrel member and terminating at its bottom end in an axial aperture; and

a writing element engaging and movable with each of said chucks and extending downwardly toward said lower barrel member bottom end.

16. A dual selectively protractable writing element writing instrument comprising:

a tubular first barrel member;

a cylindrical cam coaxially locate in said barrel member and having a cylindrical cam groove with opposite oppositely inclined cam groove sections, defined by parallel axially opposite faces;

a longitudinally stationary rotatable guide member coaxial with said cylindrical cam and having formed therein a pair of peripherally opposite longitudinally extending guideways;

a chuck member slidably engaging each of said guideways and including a transversely projection follower slideably engaging a respective cam groove section; and

a writing element coupled to each of said chucks; said writing instrument being characterized by said cylindrical cam including axially spaced coaxial first and second cam parts with said cam groove faces being defined by the confronting spaced end faces of said cam parts, said first cam part being integrally formed with said barrel member and said second cam part having mating indexing formations to provide a predetermined angular relationship between said first and second cam parts.

17. The writing instrument of claim 17 wherein said guide member is coupled to and rotatable with said lower barrel member.

18. The writing instrument of claim 17 wherein said cylindrical cam second part is integrally formed with said lower barrel member as a unitary member.

19. The writing instrument of claim 20 wherein said upper barrel member has an axial bore formed in its upper part and said guide member includes a cylindrical rod rotatably engaging said upper barrel member bore and terminating at its top in a control knob.

20. The writing instrument of claim 21 wherein said upper barrel member has an upwardly projecting sleeve coaxially formed at its top and said knob has a coaxial open bottom annular socket formed in its underface rotatably engaging said sleeve.

21. The writing instrument of claim 16 wherein said guide tracks are defined by channels of rectangular transverse cross section and each of said chuck members includes a rectangular bar slideably engaging a respective guide channel.

22. The writing instrument of claim 16 wherein each of said cam track sections extends for approximately 180 degrees.

23. The writing instrument of claim 24 wherein the lower ends of the bottom faces of said cam track sections are joined by a vertical notch.

24. The writing instrument of claim 18, the confronting peripheral faces of said first barrel member and said second cam part having mating indexing formations to provide a predetermined angular relationship between said first and second cam parts.

25. The writing instrument of claim 26 including a second barrel member coaxial with said first barrel member and integrally formed as a unit with said second cam part.

26. The writing instrument of claim 27 wherein said guide member projects axially through and is rotatable relative to said first barrel member and terminates in a knob located at the outer end of said first barrel member.

27. The writing instrument of claim 18, including a second barrel member coaxial with said first barrel member and coupled to said guide member for rotation therewith.

178

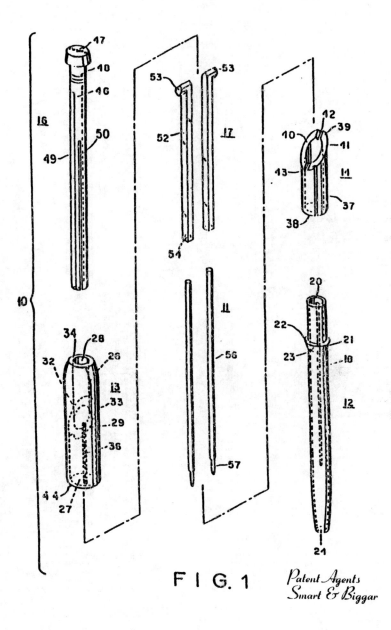

F I G. 1

Patent Agents
Smart & Biggar

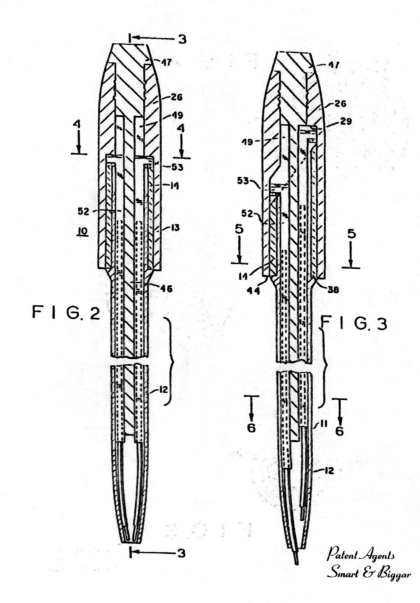

FIG. 2

FIG. 3

Patent Agents
Smart & Biggar

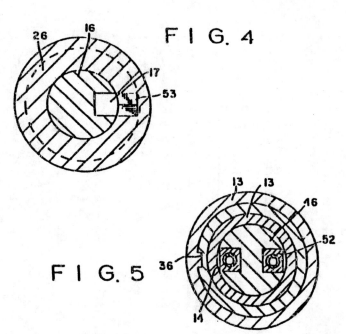

FIG. 4

FIG. 5

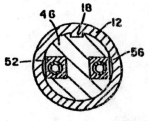

FIG. 6

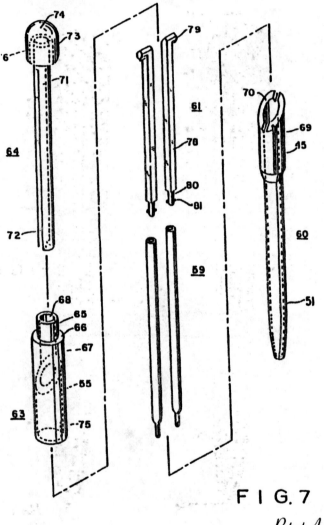

F I G. 7

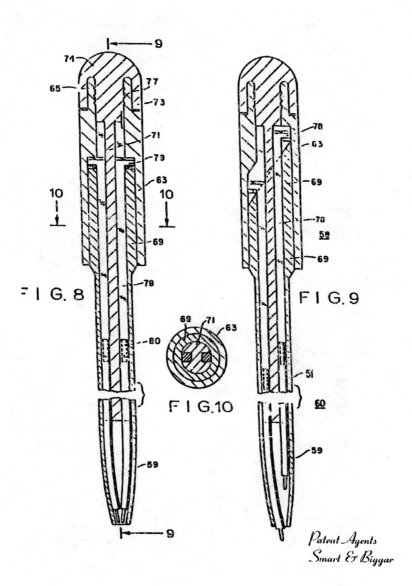

FIG. 8

FIG. 9

FIG.10

Patent Agents
Smart & Biggar

Appendix I

Members of the Paris Convention*

PARIS CONVENTION FOR THE PROTECTION OF INDUSTRIAL PROPERTY

Paris Convention of March 20, 1883, made effective July 7, 1884; revised at Brussels, December 14, 1900; revised at Washington, June 2, 1911; revised at The Hague, November 6, 1925; Revised at London, June 2, 1934; revised at Lisbon, October 31, 1958; revised at Stockholm, July 14, 1967; amended in 1979.

State	Text	Member Since
Albania	Stockholm	October 4, 1995
Algeria	Stockholm[2]	March 1, 1966
American Samoa	Stockholm	May 30, 1887
Argentina	Stockholm (A)	February 10, 1967
Armenia	Stockholm[2]	December 25, 1991
Aruba	Stockholm	July 1, 1890
Australia	Stockhoim	October 10, 1925
Austria	Stockholm	January 1, 1909
Azerbaijan	Stockholm	December 25, 1995
Azores	Stockholm	July 7, 1884
Bahamas	Stockholm (A)	October 20, 1967
Bahrain	Stockholm	October 29, 1997
Bangladesh	Stockholm (B)[2]	March 3, 1991
Barbados	Stockholm	March 12, 1985
Belarus	Stockholm[2]	December 25, 1991
Belgium	Stockholm	July 7, 1884
Benin	Stockholm	January 10, 1967
Bolivia	Stockholm	November 4, 1993
Bosnia and Herzegovina	Stockholm	March 6, 1992
Botswana	Stockholm	April 15, 1998
Brazil	Stockholm (C)[2]	July 7, 1884
Bulgaria	Stockholm[3]	June 13, 1921
Burkina Faso	Stockholm	November 19, 1963
Burundi	Stockholm	September 22, 1998
Cambodia	Stockholm	September 3, 1977

---

* The information included is effective as of January 15, 1999.

Cameroon	Stockholm	May 10, 1964
Canada	Stockholm (E)	September 1, 1923
Central African Republic	Stockholm	November 19, 1963
Chad	Stockholm	November 19, 1963
Chile	Stockholm	June 14, 1991
China	Stockholm[2]	March 19, 1985
Columbia	Stockholm	September 3, 1996
Congo	Stockholm	September 2, 1963
Costa Rica	Stockholm	October 31, 1995
Côte d'Ivoire	Stockholm	October 23, 1963
Croatia	Stockholm	October 8, 1991
Cuba	Stockholm	November 17, 1904
Cyprus	Stockholm	January 17, 1966
Czech Republic	Stockholm	January 1, 1993
Democratic People's Republic of Korea	Stockholm	June 10, 1980
Denmark[4]	Stockholm	October 1, 1894
Dominican Republic	Hague	July 11, 1890
Egypt	Stockholm[2]	July 1, 1951
El Salvador	Stockholm	February 19, 1994
Equatorial Guinea	Stockholm	June 26, 1997
Estonia	Stockholm[5]	August 24, 1994
Finland	Stockholm	September 20, 1921
France	Stockholm[6]	July 7, 1884
Gabon	Stockholm	February 29, 1964
Gambia	Stockholm	January 21, 1992
Georgia	Stockholm[2]	December 25, 1991
Germany	Stockholm	May 1, 1903
Ghana	Stockholm	September 28, 1976
Greece	Stockholm	October 2, 1924
Grenada	Stockholm	September 22, 1998
Guatemala	Stockholm[2]	August 18, 1998
Guam	Stockholm	May 30, 1887
Guinea	Stockholm	February 5, 1982
Guinea-Bissau	Stockholm	June 28, 1988
Guyana	Stockholm	October 25, 1994
Haiti	Stockholm	July 1, 1958
Hong Kong	Stockholm[8]	November 16, 1977
Holy See	Stockholm	September 29, 1960
Honduras	Stockholm	February 4, 1994
Hungary	Stockholm	January 1, 1909
Iceland	Stockholm (F)	May 5, 1962
Indonesia	Stockholm (G)	October 1, 1888
Iran (Islamic Republic of)	Lisbon	December 16, 1959
Iraq	Stockholm[2]	January 24, 1976
Ireland	Stockholm	December 4, 1925
Isle of Man	Stockholm	October 29, 1983
Israel	Stockholm	September 12, 1933

Japan	Stockholm	July 15, 1899
Jordan	Stockholm	July 17, 1972
Kazakhstan	Stockholm[2]	December 25, 1991
Kenya	Stockholm	June 14, 1965
Kyrgyzstan	Stockholm[2]	December 25, 1991
Laos	Stockholm[2]	October 8, 1998
Latvia	Stockholm[7]	September 7, 1993
Lebanon	Stockholm (D)[2]	September 1, 1924
Lesotho	Stockholm (B)[2]	September 28, 1989
Liberia	Stockholm	August 27, 1994
Libya	Stockholm	September 28, 1976
Liechtenstein	Stockholm	July 14, 1933
Lithuania	Stockholm	May 22, 1994
Luxembourg	Stockholm	June 30, 1922
Madagascar	Stockholm	December 21, 1963
Madeira	Stockholm	July 7, 1884
Malawi	Stockholm	July 6, 1964
Malaysia	Stockholm	January 1, 1989
Mali	Stockholm[2]	March 1, 1983
Malta	Stockholm (A)	October 20, 1967
Mauritania	Stockholm	April 11, 1965
Mauritius	Stockholm	September 24, 1976
Mexico	Stockholm	September 7, 1903
Monaco	Stockholm	July 30, 1917
Mongolia	Stockholm[2]	April 21, 1985
Morocco	Stockholm	August 6, 1971
Mozambique	Stockholm	July 9, 1998
Netherlands	Stockholm	July 7, 1884
Netherlands Antilles	Stockholm	July 1, 1890
New Zealand	Stockholm (D)[1]	September 7, 1891
Nicaragua	Stockholm[2]	July 3, 1996
Niger	Stockholm	July 5, 1964
Nigeria	Lisbon	September 2, 1963
Norway	Stockholm	July 1, 1885
Panama	Stockholm	October 19, 1996
Paraguay	Stockholm	May 28, 1994
Peru	Stockholm	April 11, 1995
Philippines	Stockholm[2]	September 27, 1965
Poland	Stockholm	November 10, 1919
Portugal	Stockholm	July 7, 1884
Puerto Rico (Commonwealth of)	Stockholm	May 30, 1887
Republic of Korea	Stockholm	May 4, 1980
Republic of Moldova	Stockholm[2]	December 25, 1991
Romania	Stockholm[3]	October 6, 1920
Russian Federation	Stockholm[2]	December 25, 1991
Rwanda	Stockholm	March 1, 1984
Saint Kitts and Nevis	Stockholm	April 9, 1995
Saint Lucia	Stockholm[2]	April 9, 1995

Saint Vincent and the Grenadines.	Stockholm	August 29, 1995
San Marino	Stockholm	March 4, 1960
Sao Tone and Principe	Stockholm	May 12, 1998
Senegal	Stockholm[3]	December 21, 1963
Sierra Leone	Stockholm	June 17, 1997
Singapore	Stockholm	February 23, 1995
Slovakia	Stockholm	January 1, 1993
Slovenia	Stockholm	June 25, 1991
South Africa	Stockholm	December 1, 1947
Spain	Stockholm	July 7, 1884
Sri Lanka	Stockholm (D)	December 29, 1952
Sudan	Stockholm	January 16, 1984
Suriname	Stockholm	July 1, 1890
Sweden	Stockholm	July 1, 1885
Switzerland	Stockholm[3]	July 7, 1884
Syria	Stockholm	September 1, 1924
Tajikistan	Stockholm[2]	December 25, 1991
The former Yugoslav Republic of Macedonia	Stockholm	September 8, 1991
Togo	Stockholm	September 10, 1967
Trinidad & Tobago	Stockholm	May 14, 1908
Tunisia	Stockholm	July 7, 1884
Turkey	Stockholm (H)	October 10, 1925
Uganda	Stockholm	June 14, 1965
Ukraine	Stockholm[2]	December 25, 1991
United Arab Emirates	Stockholm	September 19, 1996
United Kingdom	Stockholm	July 7, 1884
United Republic of Tanzania	Stockholm (A)	June 16, 1963
United States of America	Stockholm	May 30, 1887
Uruguay	Stockholm	March 18, 1967
Uzbekistan	Stockholm[2]	December 25, 1991
Venezuela	Stockholm	September 18, 1995
Virgin Islands	Stockholm	May 30, 1887
Vietnam	Stockholm[2]	March 8, 1949
Yugoslavia	Stockholm	February 26, 1921
Zaire	Stockholm	January 31, 1975
Zambia	Stockholm (A)	April 6, 1965
Zimbabwe	Stockholm	April 18, 1980

157 States and Dependencies

NOTES:

A   This Country is bound by Articles 13 to 30 of the Stockholm text and Articles 1 to 12 of the Lisbon text.

B   This Country is not bound by Article 28(1) of the Stockholm text.

C   This Country is bound by Articles 13 to 30 of the Stockholm text and Articles 1 to 12 of the Hague text.

D   This Country is bound by Articles 13 to 30 of the Stockholm text and Articles 1 to 12 of the London text.

E   Canada adheres to Articles 1-12 of the Stockholm text effective May 26, 1996.

F   Iceland adheres to Articles 1-12 of the Stockholm text effective April 9, 1995.

G   Indonesia adheres to Articles 1-12 of the Stockholm text effective September 5, 1997.

H   Turkey adheres to Articles 1-12 of the Stockholm text effective February 1, 1995.

1   The accession of New Zealand to the Stockholm Act, with the exception of Articles 1 to 12, extends to the Cook Islands, Niue and Tokelau.

2   With the declaration provided for in Article 28(2) of the Stockholm Act relating to the International Court of Justice.

3   There are alternative dates of entry for this state.

4   Denmark extended the application of the Stockholm Act to the Far;auoe Islands with effect from August 6, 1971.

5   Estonia acceded to the Paris Convention (Washington Act, 1911) with effect from August 20, 1925. It lost its independence on August 6, 1940 and regained it on August 21, 1991.

6   This includes all France's Overseas Departments and Territories.

7   Latvia acceded to the Paris Convention (Washington Act, 1911) with effect from August 20, 1925. It lost its independence on July 21, 1940 and regained it on August 21, 1991.

8   Effective for the Hong Kong Special Administrative Area from July 1, 1997.

Appendix J

Members of the Patent Cooperation Treaty*

PATENT COOPERATION TREATY

Patent Cooperation Treaty ("PCT") made Washington 1970; amended in 1979 and modified in 1984

State	Member Since
Albania	October 4, 1995
Armenia	December 25, 1991
Australia	March 31, 1980
Austria	April 23, 1979
Azerbaijan	December 25, 1995
Barbados	March 12, 1985
Belarus[1]	December 25, 1991
Belgium	December 14, 1981
Benin	February 26, 1987
Bosnia and Herzegovina	September 7, 1996
Brazil	April 9, 1978
Bulgaria	May 21, 1984
Burkina Faso	March 21, 1989
Cameroon	January 24, 1978
Canada	January 2, 1990
Central African Republic	January 24, 1978
Chad	January 24, 1978
China[11]	January 1, 1994
Congo	January 24, 1978
Côte d'Ivoire	April 30, 1991
Croatia	July 1, 1998
Cuba[1]	July 16, 1996
Cypress	April 1, 1998
Czech Republic	January 1, 1993

---

* The information included is effective as of March 16, 1999. The information is reproduced with the consent of the World Intellectual Property Organization ("WIPO") which administers the PCT.

Democratic People's Republic of Korea	July 8, 1980
Denmark	December 1, 1978
Estonia	August 24, 1994
Finland[2]	October 1, 1980
France[1,3]	February 25, 1978
Gabon	January 24, 1978
Gambia	December 9, 1997
Georgia[1]	December 25, 1991
Germany	January 24, 1978
Ghana	February 20, 1997
Greece[4]	October 9, 1990
Grenada	September 22, 1998
Guinea	May 27, 1991
Guinea-Bissau	December 12, 1997
Hungary[1]	June 27, 1980
Iceland	March 23, 1995
India[1]	December 7, 1998
Indonesia[1]	September 5, 1997
Ireland	August 1, 1992
Israel	June 1, 1996
Italy	March 28, 1985
Japan	October 1, 1978
Kazakhstan[1]	December 25, 1991
Kenya	June 8, 1994
Kyrgyzstan[1]	December 25, 1991
Latvia	September 7, 1993
Lesotho	October 21, 1995
Liberia	August 27, 1994
Liechtenstein[4]	March 19, 1980
Lithuania	June 5, 1994
Luxembourg	April 30, 1978
Madagascar[5]	January 24, 1978
Malawi	January 24, 1978
Mali	October 19, 1984
Mauritania	April 13, 1983
Mexico	January 1, 1995
Monaco	June 22, 1979
Mongolia	May 27, 1991
Netherlands[6]	July 10, 1979
New Zealand	December 1, 1992
Niger	March 21, 1993
Norway[2]	January 1, 1980
Poland[7]	December 25, 1990
Portugal	November 24, 1992
Republic of Korea	August 10, 1984
Republic of Moldova[1]	December 25, 1991
Romania[1]	July 23, 1979

Russian Federation[1]	December 25, 1991
Saint Lucia[1]	August 30, 1996
Senegal	January 24, 1978
Sierra Leone	June 17, 1997
Slovakia	January 1, 1993
Slovenia	March 1, 1994
South Africa[1]	March 16, 1999
Spain[4]	November 16, 1989
Sri Lanka	February 26, 1982
Sudan	April 16, 1984
Swaziland	September 20, 1994
Sweden[2]	May 17, 1978
Switzerland[4]	January 24, 1978
Tajikistan	December 25, 1991
The Former Yugoslav Republic of Macedonia	August 10, 1995
Togo	January 24, 1978
Trinidad & Tobago	March 10, 1994
Turkey	January 1, 1996
Turkmenistan[1]	December 25, 1991
Ukraine[1]	December 25, 1991
United Arab Emirates	March 10, 1999
United Kingdom[8]	January 24, 1978
United States of America[9, 10]	January 24, 1978
Uzbekistan[1]	December 25, 1991
Vietnam	March 10, 1993
Yugoslavia	February 1, 1997
Zimbabwe	June 11, 1997

100 States

NOTES:
1 With the declaration provided for in Article 64(5).
2 With the declaration provided for in Article 64(2)(a)(ii).
3 Including all overseas departments and territories.
4 With the declaration provided for in Article 64(5).
5 According to information received from the Minister for Foreign Affairs of Madagascar concerning international applications designating Madagascar, the industrial property legislation, adopted by the competent authorities, provides, among other things, for the prolongation of the time limits under Articles 22 and 39 until such time as the new patent legislation will, after its entry into force, permit the processing of patent applications in Madagascar. The said prolonged time limits will be fixed by a decree which will be promulgated in due course. The Government of Madagascar has expressed the desire that this information be conveyed to applicants using the PCT system and designating or electing Madagascar, or intending to do so, so that they may take cognizance of the possibility thus offered them validly to designate or elect Madagascar and to wait with the action required to start the national phase under Articles 22 and 39 until after the new legislation has entered into force and the time limits to be observed under it have been determined.
6 Ratification for the Kingdom in Europe, the Netherlands Antilles and Aruba.

7 With the declaration provided for in Article 64(2)(a)(i) and (ii). The declaration provided for in Article 64(2)(a)(i) was withdrawn with effect from March 1, 1994.

8 The United Kingdom extended the application of the PCT to the territory of Hong Kong with effect from April 15, 1981, and to the Isle of Man with effect from October 29, 1983.

9 With the declarations provided for in Article 64(2)(a) and 64(3)(a).

10 Extends to all areas for which the United States of America has international responsibility.

11 The Hong Kong Special Administrative Area is covered effective July 1, 1996.

INTERNATIONAL SEARCHING AUTHORITIES UNDER SECTION 16 OF THE PCT

The patent offices of Australia, Austria, China, Japan, the Russian Federation, Spain, Sweden, the United States of America, and the European Patent Office.

INTERNATIONAL PRELIMINARY EXAMINING AUTHORITIES UNDER SECTION 32 OF THE PCT

The patent offices of Australia, Austria, China, Japan, the Russian Federation, Spain, Sweden, the United Kingdom (in respect of demands for international preliminary examination made on or before May 28, 1993), the United States of America, and the European Patent Office.

Appendix K

Informal Non-Disclosure Agreement*

WHEREAS_____(the "Disclosing Party") wishes to transmit certain information, which the Disclosing Party considers valuable, proprietary and confidential, to _____, (the "Recipient"), which information relates to _____ (hereinafter the "Information").

NOW THEREFORE, in consideration of the disclosure by the Disclosing Party and the covenants contained herein, the parties hereto agree that, from the date of receipt of information identified by the the Disclosing Party as either PROPRIETARY or CONFIDEN-TIAL, the Recipient shall neither disclose it to any other person, firm or corporation nor use it for his or her own benefit except as provided herein and shall use the same degree of care to avoid publication or dissemination of such information as the Recipient employs with respect to his or her own information which it does not desire to have published or disseminated.

The Recipient shall have no obligation with respect to any such information which:

      i)   is already publicly known; or

      ii) is or becomes publicly known through no wrongful act of the Recipient; or

      iii) is approved for release by written authorization of the Disclosing Party.

[Should other limitations be considered?]

The Recipient agrees that the Information is the property of the Disclosing Party. The Recipient shall receive such Information only for the purposes of evaluation of the prospect of entering into business relations with the Disclosing Party and for no other purposes.

Nothing contained in this Non-Disclosure Agreement shall be construed as granting or conferring any rights by licence or otherwise, expressly, impliedly, or otherwise, for any invention, work of authorship, design, discovery or improvement hereafter made, conceived, or acquired prior to the date of this Agreement.

IN WITNESS WHEREOF the parties hereto have duly caused this Agreement to be executed [under seal] as of the _____ day of _____, _____.

---

* This is a model agreement supplied for illustrative purposes only. In every case you should consider the specific needs of your client's situation.

RECIPIENT   The Disclosing Party

_____   PER: _____

_____

Please print name

_____

Address

WITNESS TO RECIPIENT'S
SIGNATURE

_____

Appendix L

More Formal Non-Disclosure Agreement*

This agreement is made and entered into effective the _____ day of _____ , _____ by ABC Ltd. having a place of business at _____ (hereinafter "ABC"), and XYZ Ltd. having a place of business at _____ (hereinafter "XYZ").

NON-DISCLOSURE AGREEMENT

This agreement provides for the disclosure by ABC to XYZ of valuable proprietary and confidential Information of ABC. Accordingly, in consideration of the disclosure of Information and to provide protection for ABC's Information, the parties hereto agree as follows:

1.   The Parties enter into this agreement to permit ABC to provide to XYZ Information solely to conduct discussions and negotiations towards the establishment of a potential business relationship regarding _____ under terms that will protect the confidential nature of such Information. XYZ is prohibited from using the Information of ABC for any purpose other than those identified above without first obtaining the express written permission of ABC.

2.   "Information" shall mean information, whether disclosed in writing, orally or otherwise, of any nature in any form including drawings, specifications, data, graphs, charts, business plans, designs, research, software, trade secrets, processes, compositions, techniques, compilations, discoveries, improvements, inventions, ideas, know how, flow charts, marketing plans and any other technical, business or financial information which is developed or disclosed for the purpose of this agreement. Where practical ABC may have the information identified as "Proprietary" or "Confidential" with an appropriate legend, marking, stamp, or other obvious written identification.

3.   "Intellectual Property" shall mean any industrial or intellectual property rights including, without limitation, rights to any inventions, discoveries, improvements, patents, patent applications, copyright, trademarks, integrated circuit topography or mask works, Information, designs, whether registered or not and all such other rights which may be recognized under law, equity or otherwise, to protect technical or other creative contributions or expressions.

---

*   This is a model agreement supplied for illustrative purposes only. In every case you should consider the specific needs of your client's situation.

4. Upon receiving Information, XYZ shall keep in confidence and not disclose to any person or entity, any of the Information, except as otherwise provided by the terms and conditions of this agreement. XYZ shall exercise the highest standard of care to present disclosure or improper use of such information if required by ABC. XYZ shall bring all action necessary to oppose or improper use any disclosure of Information by XYZ or any of its employees or consultants.

5. XYZ shall not be liable for the disclosure or use of specific Information if the same is:

    (a)   developed by XYZ independent of any disclosure hereunder as evidenced by written records; or

    (b)   disclosed with prior written approval of ABC.

    [Consider if additional limits on the obligations are acceptable.]

6. XYZ shall make the Information available only to those of its employees or any Recipient having a "need to know" only for the purposes of the business review contemplated under this agreement. XYZ shall cause its employees, or any Recipient to enter into a Non-disclosure Agreement providing similar restrictions as in this agreement and which agreement shall be for the benefit of ABC and enforceable at the option of ABC.

    "Recipient" shall mean any individual, firm, partnership, body corporate, association, government or other entity which ABC, at the request of XYZ, has given approval, in writing, to have access to the Information and who has entered into a non-disclosure Agreement satisfactory to ABC.

7. XYZ shall advise each of its employees, or any Recipient participating in the business review contemplated under this agreement, that they are obligated to protect the Information in a manner consistent with this agreement and shall supervise their use of Information to ensure they do so.

8. Notwithstanding any provision of this agreement, all right, title and interest, whether at law, in equity or otherwise, in any Information or Intellectual Property disclosed by ABC or developed by XYZ shall be and remain the property of ABC. All analysis, compilations, data, studies, notes, summaries or other documents prepared by XYZ, its employees or any Recipient, containing or based upon, in whole or in part, the Information or any part of it disclosed by ABC shall be the property of ABC and shall form part of the Information of ABC for the purposes of this agreement.

9. To the extent XYZ or its employees, contractors or agents jointly create any Intellectual Property based, related, derived from in whole or in part from or on the Information or any of it or make any other extension, improvement, modification or discovery related in any way to the ABC compound, process or technology then XYZ shall assign all such Intellectual Property to ABC.

10. All Information shall remain the property of ABC and all written Information shall be returned to ABC or destroyed by XYZ, when requested by ABC at any time, or when XYZ's need for such information for the purpose of this agreement has ended, whichever is earlier. In the event of destruction, XYZ shall certify in writing to ABC, within thirty (30) days that such destruction has been accomplished.

198

XYZ shall make no further use of such Information.

11. The disclosure of Information hereunder shall not be construed as granting either a licence under any patent, patent application or other Intellectual Property or any right of ownership in said Information. Nor shall such disclosure constitute any representation, warranty, assurance, guarantee, or inducement by ABC with respect to infringement of patents or other rights of third parties.

12. The obligations and responsibilities of the parties hereto shall survive and continue in full force and effect beyond the termination of this agreement for any cause.

13. The effective date of this agreement shall be _____and shall continue until terminated by the written agreement of the Parties.

14. This agreement contains the entire understanding between the parties with respect to the safeguarding of said Information and supersedes all prior communications and understandings with respect thereto. No waiver, alteration, modification, or amendment shall be binding or effective for any purpose whatsoever unless and until reduced to writing and executed by authorized representatives of the parties.

15. This agreement shall be construed in accordance with the laws of the Province of _____, and Canada and the Parties attorn to the jurisdiction of the courts in _____ for the purpose of this agreement.

16. If any provision of this agreement is declared invalid, illegal or unenforceable by a Court of competent jurisdiction such provision shall be severed from the agreement and all other provisions of the agreement shall remain in full force and effect.

17. This agreement and the rights and obligations hereunder may not be assigned by XYZ without the prior written consent of ABC.

18. The Parties confirm that the purpose of this agreement is to provide a framework for disclosure of valuable Information of ABC to XYZ. The Parties agree that breach of the provisions of this agreement may cause irreparable harm to ABC which harm may not be adequately compensable by monetary damages and accordingly, in the event of breach of this agreement ABC shall be entitled to obtain injunctive relief in any court of competent jurisdiction for the purpose of enforcing the provisions of this agreement and more specifically to restrain any disclosure or use of Information or Intellectual Property contrary to the provisions of this agreement. ABC shall not be required to post a bond for the purpose of obtaining any such injunctive relief. The injunctive relief shall be in addition to any other remedy ABC may be entitled to receive in law or in equity.

19. ABC makes no representation or warranty as to the accuracy or the completeness of the Information and shall have no liability, direct or indirect, to XYZ as a result of any use or evaluation of the Information by XYZ. Only those particular representations and warranties, if any, which may be made in a definitive agreement, if as and when it may be executed, subject to such limitations and restrictions as may be specified in such definitive agreement, shall have any legal effect as between the parties.

20. This Agreement may be executed by the Parties in counterparts.

THIS AGREEMENT MADE BY THE PARTIES HERETO AS EVIDENCED BY THE EXECUTION BY THEIR OFFICERS HEREUNTO DULY AUTHORIZED.

XYZ LTD.   ABC LTD.

Per: _____   Per: _____

Name: _____   Name: _____

Title: _____   Title: _____

Date: _____   Date: _____

Appendix M

Trade Secret Law and Non-Disclosure Agreements

This appendix provides an introduction to trade secret law (Part I) and a checklist of issues to consider in non-disclosure agreements (Part II).

PART I — INTRODUCTION TO THE LAW OF TRADE SECRETS

Information, data, ideas, plans, designs or concepts, whether technical or business in nature, may be protected under trade secret law.[1] Historically the chancellor had jurisdiction over a person's conscience and provided relief when strict application of the common law would lead to injustice. Over time courts of chancery were established and administered a system of discretionary remedies known as equity. Among those remedies was the ability of the court to bind a person's conscience to require him to maintain secret information in confidence. That is the historical basis of the protection of trade secrets and other forms of confidential information.[2]

The action to enforce these rights became known as the breach of confidence action.[3] Note that obligations of confidence may also arise under contract (in which case there may be rights under equity and rights under the contract).

The breach of confidence action gives the person to whom the obligation of confidence is owed the right to require the person who owes the obligation to keep the information secret. In many non-disclosure agreements or as a result of the particular relationship these restrictions are extended to include a restriction on use of the confidential information.

The elements of the breach of confidence action include a relationship of confidence, specific confidential information and detriment arising from disclosure. These elements are discussed below, as follows:

---

[1] Other forms of intellectual property protection may also be applicable. For an introduction see *Canadian Intellectual Property Law in a Nutshell*, (Toronto: Carswell, 1998).

[2] See, for further background, *Saltman Engineering Co. v. Campbell Engineering Co.* (1948), 65 R.P.C. 203 (Eng. C.A.); and *Seager v. Copydex Ltd.* [1967] 1 W.L.R. 923, [1967] 2 All E.R. 415 (C.A.) and the cases cited therein.

[3] For the most current review of the breach of confidence action and remedies see *Cadbury Schweppes Inc. v. FBI Foods Ltd.*, (1999), 167 D.L.R. (4th) 577 (S.C.C.).

(1) A RELATIONSHIP OF CONFIDENCE

There must be an obligation of confidence owed in relation to the specific confidential information. As a result there must be a relationship between the person who owns the confidential information and the person who is to be bound by the obligation of confidence. The obligation of confidence may arise from a variety of relationships, including:

    i.   An express obligation of confidence such as in a non-disclosure agreement;[4]

    ii.   Implied obligations of confidence as may arise:

        1. In circumstances where there is an obligation of confidence implied such as, for example, during pre-contractual negotiations.[5]

        2. In circumstances where the obligation of confidence is implied by law, such as in a fiduciary relationship.[6]

Sometimes employees are also bound either by obligations in their relationship with the employer sometimes characterized as fiduciary obligations.[7]

A fiduciary (such as a director or senior officer) is precluded from obtaining for him or herself, either secretly or without the approval of the company, any property or business advantage belonging to the company or for which it has been negotiating.[8] Note that an employee can not disclose confidential information of the employer.[9]

Sometimes the courts appear to confuse the requirement for an obligation of confidence with the higher requirements of a fiduciary relationship. For example, in *International Corona Resources Ltd. v. Lac Minerals Ltd.*[10] some of the Justices of the Supreme Court of Canada found a fiduciary relationship to exist between two mining companies in pre-contractual negotiations. It is clear that a fiduciary relationship is not required to sustain a breach of confidence action.[11]

(2) CONFIDENTIAL INFORMATION

In order for there to be an obligation of confidence the information must be confidential.[12] As a result any publication or disclosure of the specific information would make the information available to the public. This must be considered when making patent

---

[4] See, for example, *Eli Lilly Canada Inc. v. Shamrock Chemicals. Ltd.* (1985), 6 C.I.P.R. 5 (Ont. H.C.). See the discussion in part II of this appendix for a discussion of common terms in non-disclosure agreements.

[5] See, for example, *Seager v. Copydex Ltd.* [1967] 1 W.L.R. 923, 2 All E.R. 415 (C.A.); *International Corona Resources Ltd. v. Lac Minerals Ltd.* [1989] 44 B.L.R. 1 (S.C.C.). In each such case there were circumstances suggesting the existence of obligations of confidence.

[6] See, for example, *Boardman v. Phipps* [1967] 2 A.C. 46 (U.K. H.L.)

[7] See *Hivac Ltd. v. Park Royal Scientific Instruments Ltd.* [1946] 1 Ch. 169 (Eng. C.A.) and *Chevron Standard Ltd. v. Home Oil Co.* (1980), 50 C.P.R. (2d) 182 (Alta. Q.B.) affirmed (1982), 64 C.P.R. (2d) 11 (Alta. C.A.).

[8] *Canadian Aero Service Ltd. v. O'Malley* (1973), 11 C.P.R. (2d) 206 (S.C.C.)

[9] *Scapa Dryers (Can.) Ltd. v. Fardeau* (1971) 1 C.P.R. (2d) 199 (Que. S.C.).

[10] *Supra*, note 5.

[11] See *Cadbury Schweppes Inc., supra*, note 3.

[12] *Saltman Engineering Co. Ltd. supra*, note 2; *Shauenburg Industries Ltd. v. Borowski* (1979), 50 C.P.R. (2d) 69 (Ont. H.C.).

applications or seeking other forms of protection where the application, or if granted, the registration, is available to the public. Other examples of disclosures which would preclude protection include: publication of the information in an article or brochure, public use, sale of a product embodying the information or from which the information may be extracted.

Note that the confidential information may be knowledge of the intent of another party in respect of information which is available to the public.[13]

(3) UNAUTHORIZED USE OR DISCLOSURE TO THE DETRIMENT OF THE DISCLOSER

In order to be actionable the unauthorized use or disclosure must be to the detriment of the owner of the confidential information.[14] This is usually not difficult for the plaintiff to show since loss of control over the information usually is to the detriment of the owner.[15] This can result in loss of the head start associated with knowledge and control of the information.[16]

It is actionable if a person who owes an obligation of confidence, without the consent of the owner of the confidential information, discloses or misuses the confidential information or any part thereof.[17] The full range of remedies are available for violation of a breach of confidence.[18]

In the case of an innocent third party who acquires the confidential information without notice of the breach of the obligation of confidence but is subsequently informed of the breach is also bound by the obligation of confidence so long as the information is not yet published.[19]

The equitable nature of the breach of confidence action gives rise to unique limits on the action. Given the equitable basis of the obligation of confidence it is critical that there be a relationship between the owner of the confidential information and the person who is to be bound by the obligation of confidence. The requirement for a relationship means that the rights involved in the protection of confidential information are only *in*

---

[13] *International Corona Resources Ltd. supra*, note 5.

[14] *Ibid.*

[15] A discussion of some forms of detriment may also be found in *Cadbury Schweppes Inc. supra*, note 3.

[16] *Chevron Standard Ltd.* supra, note 7.

[17] See, for example, *Coco v. A.N. Clark (Engineers) Ltd.* (1968), [1969] R.P.C. 41 (Eng. Ch. Div.); *Slavutych v. Baker* (1975), [1976] 1 S.C.R. 254 (S.C.C.); and *R.L. Crain Ltd. v. Ashton* [1949] O.R. 303 (Ont. H.C.); affirmed [1950] O.R. 62 (Ont. C.A.). *Cadbury Schweppes Inc.* supra, note 3 suggests even more flexible remedies may also be available.

[18] A very common form of relief is an interlocutory injunction and then permanent injunction, see *International Tools Ltd. v. Kollar* (1968), 67 D.L.R. (2d) 386 (Ont C.A.). Other forms of relief available include: (a) damages, see *Seager v. Copydex Ltd.* (No. 2), [1969] 2 All E.R. 718 (Eng. C.A.), *Shauenburg Industries Ltd.* supra, note 12; (b) an account of profits, see *Peter Pan Manufacturing Corp. v. Corsets Silhouette Ltd.* [1963] 3 All E.R. 402 (Eng. Ch. Div.); (c) a constructive trust, see *Pre-Cam Exploration & Development Ltd. v. McTavish* [1966] S.C.R. 551 (S.C.C.); and (d) an order for delivery-up, see *International Corona Resources Ltd.* supra, note 5.

[19] See, for example, *Wheatly v. Bell* [1984] F.S.R. 16 (N.S.W. S.C.). This principle is adopted in *Cadbury Schweppes Inc.* supra, note 3.

personam, not *in rem*. This is a considerable limit on the protection available under trade secret law. As a result some kinds of industrial espionage activity may not be caught by this action.[20]

Other limits on this cause of action include: (a) loss of confidence;[21] (b) just cause or excuse;[22] (c) disclosure required by law such as in legal proceedings, in investigation by a regulatory body,[23] securities regulation, in patent applications and like applications; and (d) any of the equitable remedies.

PART II — SPECIFIC ISSUES IN BASIC NON-DISCLOSURE AGREEMENTS

As previously discussed, a very common means of establishing a relationship of confidence is to use a Non-Disclosure Agreement ("NDA") (also known as a Confidentiality Agreement, Secrecy Agreement or by several other names). Such an agreement provides tangible evidence of the existence of the obligations of confidence as well as defining specific issues in respect of the scope of the relationship. The following discussion introduces a number of the key points in a basic NDA. Obviously, additional points will also arise from time to time and there has been a trend to add broader commercial terms into an NDA. Some aspects of this phenomena are discussed under Part III, below.

FORM OF AGREEMENT

The essential elements of an NDA can typically be provided in a document of one to two pages. In many situations such brevity is desired as it facilitates establishing a clean relationship in a timely manner. Obviously, however, a shorter document tends to provide less certainty in respect of other commercial or other issues and so some NDA's seek to expand on the essential terms by adding additional terms to further define the relationship. Ultimately, the decision of the degree of formality of an NDA is a matter of business judgment and style weighing some of the advantages of an informal shorter document versus the greater certainty provided in respect of the more formal NDA.

An NDA may be one sided or mutual. A one sided NDA deals with the disclosure of confidential information from one party to the other party. A mutual NDA deals with a situation where both parties will disclose confidential information to each other. The following terms are discussed in the context of a one sided NDA but appropriate adjustment should also be contemplated for a mutual NDA.

---

[20] See, for example, *Franklin v. Giddins* [1978] 7d R. 72 (Brisbane S.C.); See also *R. v. Stewart* (1982) 68 C.C.C. (2d) 305 (Ont. H.C.), reversed (1983), 5 C.C.C. (3d) 481 (Ont. C.A.), reversed (1988), 41 C.C.C (3d) 481 (S.C.C.) in which the Supreme Court held that confidential information was not property for the purposes of the *Criminal Code* theft provision and therefore could not be stolen since there was no deprivation. For a critique of this decision see *A Review of Canada's Computer Crime and Computer Abuse Laws*, (1990) 7:12 C.C.L.R. 125 and 8:1 C.C.L.R. 1.

[21] See, for example, *Attorney General v. Times Newspapers Ltd.* [1973] 3 All E.R. 54 (U.K. H.L.).

[22] See, for example, *Canadian Javelin Ltd. v. Sparling* (1978), 4 B.L.R. 153 (Fed. T.D.); and *Lennon v. News Group Newspapers Ltd.* [1978] F.S.R. 573 (N.S.W. C.A.).

[23] See, for example, *Competition Act*, S.C. 1986, c. 26; *National Energy Board Act*, R.S.C. 1985, c. N-6; *Investment Canada Act*, S.C. 1985, c. 20

PARTIES

It is critically important to identify the parties to the transaction. In particular, the disclosing party needs to know who will be bound by the obligations of confidence. In this regard it is important to differentiate between individuals to whom the disclosure is made and a corporation, firm or other institution who may be bound by the obligations. A related issue is that of legal capacity of the signing party to bind an entity for which he purports to sign. While ostensible authority would typically be raised, query whether such an argument is effective where a very junior individual in an organization signs on behalf of the organization.

Obviously, it is important to verify the proper identity, legal name and address of the parties. In many short-form NDA's, the address provided as part of the definition of the parties is the only identification of a means by which to communicate should the need arise.

From the perspective of the receiving party it is important to understand who the disclosing party is (again, whether an individual, firm, corporation or other entity) so as to be able to both define the obligation and perform it to that party properly.

SCOPE OF INFORMATION

Many NDA's define, in general terms, the type of information which is being disclosed. This is desirable where a specific NDA is being entered into, for example, for review of a specific technology, review of a specific business opportunity, etc. The parties should appreciate, however, that a narrower definition of the scope of information disclosed may or may not, depending on the drafting of the agreement, limit the obligations between the parties in respect of other confidential information disclosed outside the scope of that relationship.

PURPOSE OF THE DISCLOSURE

Many NDA's define an activity or a specific purpose for which the confidential information is being disclosed. This is desirable as it seeks to limit the possible uses or purposes to which the confidential information may be put. The provision of such an activity or purpose is also used in defining the scope of use restriction, discussed below.

DEFINITION OF INFORMATION

Many NDA's contain a broad definition of "proprietary information", "information", "confidential information", "trade secrets" or some other term. That definition often contains operative terms that are of significance to the parties. Some of those operative terms are discussed in further headings, below.

From the perspective of the definition, some of the issues are a coverage of a broad class of information and whether or not the form in which information is expressed or communicated (i.e. written, oral, by demonstration) is relevant. Most definitions will include a broader attempt to define classes of information (which may include technical information, business information, financial information, test results, etc.).

It is important that both sides to the NDA review carefully the type and form of information to be protected. One should be aware particularly of any limitations to the type of information which is communicated, unless there are special reasons for such limitations, as such matters are likely to lead to future dispute, misunderstanding or conflict between the parties.

REQUIREMENTS FOR FORMALITY

Some NDA's require (often in the form of the definition of "Confidential Information") certain formalities in order to provide for protection of confidential information. Such formality might require, for example, that confidential information only includes information which is clearly marked "proprietary" or "confidential" or, if disclosed orally, is reduced to writing within a specific period of time (say, for example, 15 days from the oral disclosure) then the information must be described in specific detail in a writing and marked "proprietary" or "confidential".

The purpose of this formality seeks to both provide greater certainty of what specific information is covered by the obligations and exclude informal, casual or similar disclosures of confidential information from the obligations of confidence which arise under the agreement.

The use of such formalities is very desirable from the perspective of the receiving party who wishes to define, with some precision, the specific information which is bound by the obligations of confidence. From the disclosing party, however, the use of formalities imposes substantial requirement to ensure compliance with the formal process and to follow-up, particularly in the case of the informal or oral disclosures, which need to be reduced to writing within a particular time-frame.

Such clauses are typically coupled with a term or covenant that the receiving party owes no obligations in respect of confidential information it receives except as specifically provided in the agreement. The effect of such term is to seek to preclude any obligation in respect of informally disclosed confidential information. This is obviously a considerable risk to the disclosing party and would need to be evaluated and managed by the disclosing party in determining how much information to disclose, under what circumstances and what protections to put in place for the confidential information. For example a disclosing party may choose to specially train individuals who will be involved in the disclosure process to not stray from a prepared script or previously recorded written disclosures.

Other cautions would be to avoid any probing in areas outside pre-existing written disclosures. Obviously, a second procedural caution in respect of these types of arrangements deals with the requirement, if imposed, to mark confidential information as "proprietary" or "confidential" or require some other specific marking. It is obvious that failure to comply with this procedural requirement may be of substantial detriment to the disclosing party. As a result, the disclosing party will need to ensure that it has adequate procedures in place to identify and mark all applicable disclosures and confidential information with the necessary markings.

Some companies establish a practice of marking all documents containing any confidential information (for example placing headers, footers or the like on every page of a document warning of the confidentiality of the content). Other companies may have a special stamp prepared so that they can stamp appropriate documents with a confidential or proprietary legend.

Such footers, headers, stamps or other marking mechanisms can easily be adapted to also include a formal copyright notice as well. While there is no requirement in Canada, for such a marking or notice to create the copyright, nonetheless the placement of such a notice is helpful in cautioning regarding the copyright ownership claim. Further, proper copyright notices may also permit the creation of rights under international treatise.

NON-DISCLOSURE OBLIGATION AND RESTRICTIONS ON USE

Most NDAs provide for both obligations of confidence as well as restrictions on use of the confidential information for purposes other than the indicated activity.

It is important to review an NDA to see that it addresses both of these issues.

The obligation of confidence is, of course, fundamental to the creation of the right under trade secret law.

The issue regarding restriction on use of the confidential information is an enhancement of traditional trade secret law principles and seeks to address the fact that in many situations one may be able to benefit from knowledge of confidential information without actually disclosing the information to another (for example where the confidential information might constitute a secret process, not disclosed through an examination of the resulting product made from that process, one would not be disclosing the confidential information by practicing the process).

The disclosing party will be very concerned to ensure that there is a restriction precluding unauthorized disclosure and use of the confidential information. The receiving party will wish to ensure that the scope of permitted activity is broad enough to contemplate what is actually intended by the parties so as to avoid incidental or unintended breach of the NDA.

SCOPE OF THE DUTY

A significant advantage of an NDA is the ability to define, with some certainty, the scope of the obligations of confidence. This obligation is commonly satisfied if the receiving party performs to a defined standard. Some standards found in NDA's, depending on the circumstances, would include:

(a)   an obligation to keep confidential information strictly confidential;

(b)   an obligation to use reasonable care in keeping confidential information confidential:

      (i) sometimes the standard of care is defined as that which the receiving party uses for its own confidential information it does not wish disclosed or disseminated; or

      (ii) sometimes the standard is defined as the degree of care taken by the receiving party for its own confidential information provided that this is no less than reasonable care; or

(c)   all reasonable precautions to protect the confidentiality of the information (although this approach is often criticized because the term "all" could pose a very high duty to investigate and determine what precautions might be available).

PERMITTED DISCLOSURE TO OTHERS

Often the receiving party must disclose the confidential information which it receives under the NDA to its own employees or, possibly, third party contractors, in order to carry out the contemplated activity. Some NDA's provide a procedure regulating such disclosures to other parties or individuals.

Some NDA's restrict disclosure in the receiving party on a "need to know" basis so that the receiving party has a further duty to monitor and manage the extent to which the confidential information is disclosed within the organization.

In respect of disclosure to employees, some (few) NDA's require an additional process involving each individual employee to sign a form of NDA acceptable to the disclosing party. Because this imposes an administrative and procedural burden on the receiving party, it is common that a receiving party will seek to resist such an obligation. What the disclosing party is seeking to do in such a circumstance is to create a direct contractual and equitable relationship with each individual who has access to the confidential information so that the disclosing party has the ability, if needed, to promptly bring enforcement action against threatened or actual breach without having to ask through an intermediary stage, such as dealing with the receiving party. Most receiving parties do not wish such potential for interference with their employees and prefer to manage breaches by their employees internally and therefore would seek to resist creating direct contractual or other relationship by the other employees directly to the disclosing party.

A further factor often found in NDA's is a requirement that the receiving party provide instructions, either orally or in written form, to any employees or others who receive the confidential information to caution of the confidential and restricted nature of that information.

Most NDA's prohibit disclosure to third parties including subcontractors. A typical view of a disclosing party would be that the subcontractor should have a direct contractual connection to the disclosing party. Disclosing parties tend to be less willing to accommodate disclosures to such third parties than, for example, in the case of disclosure to employees within the receiving party where, obviously the receiving party has much greater control and ability to supervise the employee and exercise more forceful disciplinary and other actions, if required. In some cases, however, it is not practical to seek to create individual contractual arrangements with a large number of potential contractors and the disclosing party may, in the circumstances, be satisfied with the covenant of the receiving party to be responsible for the liability associated with any wrongful disclosure by any such third parties.

A further alternative, in some cases, is that the receiving party will covenant that it will have an obligation of confidence restrictions on use in its relationship with the third party sufficient to provide a mechanism to protect the confidential information (usually to the same level as provided in the NDA itself).

DURATION OF THE OBLIGATIONS

Some, but not all, NDA's provide that the obligations and restrictions in the agreement terminate on the expiration of a particular time (often measured from the date of disclosure or date of signing the agreement). Since the obligations of secrecy can be legally enforceable indefinitely, provided that the information is maintained as secret, such a limitation in an NDA places the particular confidential information, so disclosed, at risk of not being legally protectable beyond the stated time period.

Obviously, it will be important for the disclosing party to have alternative forms of protection (i.e. patent protection, copyright protection, etc.) in place prior to expiration of that time period.

From a disclosing party's perspective and because confidential information can theoretically endure indefinitely, the disclosing party will wish no time limit to exist. The receiving party, on the other hand, may for administrative purposes wish to have some certainty about when its obligations in respect of often vague and ill-defined confidential information (for example, oral disclosures for which there may be little or no evidence) have ended.

COMMON LIMITATIONS OR EXCLUSIONS FROM THE OBLIGATIONS

Many NDA's provide for a number of exceptions or limitations on the obligations of confidence and restrictions of use provided in the agreement. Fundamental to many of these exclusions is the principle that if others have unrestricted access to the information then the receiving party should not be in a worse position by having entered into the Non-Disclosure Agreement.

Other issues which are sought to be addressed by these exceptions deal with the likely possibility that the disclosing party already knows the confidential information whereas working on similar projects and wishes to prevent its own research and development activities, confidential business opportunities and the like from being "tainted" by receiving the confidential information from the disclosing party and being restrained from using what the receiving party believes it has already developed.

Typical exclusions might include:

(a)   if the information is in the public domain (i.e. available without restriction to others generally);

(b)   if the information is made available by the disclosing party to a third party without similar restrictions on disclosure or use (because the receiving party will not wish to be in a worse position than the third party);

(c)   if the information questioned is subsequently made available to the public without such disclosure being as a result of a breach of the NDA by the receiving party (for example, as a result of actions by the disclosing party, as a result of sale of products incorporating the confidential information, etc.); and

(d)   if the information in question is already known to or is developed by the receiving party without access to the confidential information provided by the disclosing party. Such an exception typically requires proof of such an allegation either to the reasonable satisfaction of the disclosing party or as may be required by a court of competent jurisdiction;

(e)   disclosure required by law such as regulatory proceedings, securities filings, etc. although some NDA's provide that if a court or regulatory body requests disclosure of the confidential information, then the receiving party may be obligated to notify disclosing party who may then seek a protective order.

RETURN OF THE INFORMATION

Many NDA's provide that, on request by the disclosing party, the receiving party will return tangible embodiments including the confidential information which may be in the possession or control of the receiving party. Obviously, the receiving party cannot return the "ideas or information", but can return the physical form in which the ideas or information are expressed.

Some NDA's provide that on the end of the relationship the receiving party will destroy the confidential information and will certify such destruction by a certificate signed by a duly authorized officer of the receiving party. This approach is commonly used in "shrink-wrap" or similar mass market software licence agreements.

Some receiving parties reserve a right for their legal department to retain a copy of the confidential information in order to deal with a potential future dispute regarding the existence or compliance with the obligations under the NDA. Such provisions typically provide that the material will be kept on the lawyer's file and used only for such restricted purposes.

NO IMPLIED LICENCE

In order to avoid any doubt about the temporary or limited nature of the rights provided under the NDA, some NDA's go on to indicate that no right or licence in the confidential information itself or any underlying intellectual property rights, technology or business opportunities are implied by the NDA.

EXECUTION PROVISIONS

Some NDA's provide that the agreement is executed under seal (and also provide for legal seals to be affixed to the document) as a substitute for consideration. Normally, the consideration is stated to be the receiving party's agreement to the restrictions in exchange for having access to the confidential information. Where there may be some doubt the addition of a seal is sought to provide an enforceable deed.

Obviously the signing parties should be identified, authorized and should execute, as applicable, the agreement. Some NDA's are compared in a unilateral form so that the obligations are created only requiring the recipient to sign the agreement. In some unilateral NDA's of that type the covenants also include not only the obligation, but an undertaking to keep the confidential information confidential, not disclose it or use it for other than the purposes provided in the NDA.

PART III — SPECIAL TERMS

A number of NDA's are enhanced by additional terms in an effort to further clarify or define, with certainty, the relationship of the parties. Some of the special terms which might be added are discussed below.

GOVERNING LAW

Rather than rely on the general law providing for jurisdiction of courts in dealing with the agreement (such as place of execution, etc.) some NDA's provide for a governing law clause. Further, some NDA's provide for attornment and occasionally exclusive jurisdiction for a particular court to address violations of the agreement.

Where the NDA purports to be governed by a law other than Alberta law, of course, the domestic law governing the NDA should be reviewed to determine the adequacy and scope of that law's ability to protect confidential information.

Because of the highly litigious environment in the United States, many Canadian parties seek to avoid being subject to U.S. law jurisdiction. This is particularly the case because of the broader scope for punitive damages can be awarded by some U.S. courts. The issue of how a U.S. court may take jurisdiction (e.g. under the "long arm" statutes in many states) and interaction with choice of law clauses is beyond the scope of this paper. Many Canadian parties also resist exclusive jurisdiction provisions providing for sole jurisdiction to resolve the dispute in a US court.

IMPROVEMENTS AND SUGGESTIONS

It is not unusual that once the recipient has the confidential information it may cause the recipient to come up with additional ideas, improvements or enhancements of the original confidential information. A question arises who should own or have rights to such further information and any intellectual property rights that might be contained therein.

Without the NDA, and ignoring, for the time being, any obligations of secrecy or the fact that the information which originally promoted the creation of the improvements came from another party, the creator of the improvements is likely to have a claim to ownership of those improvements. The basic theory is that the creator should be rewarded for his or her efforts and in particular the creativity they exercise should be encouraged. The concern of a disclosing party in these circumstances is that improvements made by the recipient may impair the disclosing party's ability to continue to develop its business and may in effect require the disclosing party and receiving party to enter into a business combination to prevent a future dispute or the disclosing party's continued development of its own confidential information. To avoid this problem, some NDA's provide that ideas, suggestions and improvements made by the receiving party become the property of the disclosing party and the receiving party agrees to assign those to the disclosing party and sign necessary documents to accomplish that result.

Some disclosing parties object on the basis that if substantial improvements are made, considerable value may be transferred to the disclosing party without any corresponding compensation. Sometimes this issue is resolved by providing for a limited period of review and where the receiving party makes no deliberate effort to make improvements or suggestions to the confidential information until or unless there is a more definitive agreement between the parties. In other words, the receiving party, in such circumstances, will seek to carry out only a preliminary evaluation with the view of determining if there is sufficient merit to enter into a more definitive agreement. The definitive agreement would address issues of ownership and control of any improvements.

INJUNCTIVE RELIEF

The granting of injunctive relief for breach or threatened breach of the obligations of an NDA is an equitable remedy subject to the traditional requirements imposed by the courts for granting of such extraordinary relief. Notwithstanding that this is a discretionary remedy and that there are few judges who would wish to see their discretion restricted, some NDA's provide specific clauses under which a disclosing party extracts an agreement from the receiving party that the disclosing party is entitled to injunctive relief in the event of breach or threatened breach of the provisions of the NDA.

Some clauses of this type go further and indicate that the disclosing party would not be obligated to post a bond in order to obtain such relief (one of the traditional requirements for granting injunctive relief). It is yet to be seen where a judge feels that his or her discretion to grant (or deny) injunctive relief is impinged by such a clause. On the other hand it can also not be shown in how many cases the existence of such a clause may have assisted a judge to feel more comfortable in granting injunctive relief in the case of breach or threatened breach.

The issue of injunctive relief is a critical concern to the disclosing party because, as noted in the description of trade secret law, if the potential breach or threatened breach can be stopped before the information becomes available to the public without restriction, then the trade secret protection can be preserved. On the other hand, once the information flows into the public domain, then all secrecy protection in respect of that specific information is lost. The disclosing party's remedy, at that stage, is limited to damages which may be an inappropriate form of remedy.

INDEMNITY

In addition to the rights obtained under the general law for breach or violation of the agreement, some NDA's provide for further indemnity by the receiving party to hold harmless and indemnify the disclosing party in respect of any damages it suffers as a result of the breach of the provisions of the NDA by the receiving party. Obviously, seeking such an indemnity is fundamentally premised on the underlying resisting presumption of solvency of the receiving party and its ability to make good on such a covenant.

STANDSTILL ARRANGEMENT

For NDA agreements that address the disclosure of confidential information with a view to possible business transactions, some NDA's provide for an agreement not to negotiate competing or conflicting arrangements during an evaluation period. It is critical in standstill arrangements that the specific restrictions are clearly defined both in terms of what might constitute negotiations and what parties such negotiations cannot be carried out with.

Appendix N

References

PATENTS

Barrigar. *Canadian Patent Act Annotated*. 2nd Edition. Canada Law Book, 1994.
CIPO. *A Guide to Patents*. Industry Canada, 1998.
Fox. *The Canadian Law and Practice Relating to Letters Patent for Inventions*. Carswell, 1969.
Henderson. *Patent Law of Canada*. Carswell, 1994.
Fox's Patent Cases. 22 volumes. Carswell, 1994.
Hughes and Woodley On Patents. Looseleaf. Butterworths, 1984.
Kratz. *Canadian Intellectual Property Law*. Carswell, 1998.
Terrell On the Law of Patents. Edition 14. Sweet & Maxwell, 1994.

TRADE-MARKS

CIPO. *A Guide to Trade-Marks*. Industry Canada, 1998.
Henderson. *Trade-Marks Law of Canada*. Carswell, 1993.
Hughes On Trademarks. Looseleaf. Butterworths, 1984.
Kratz. *Canadian Intellectual Property Law*. Carswell, 1998.
Kerly's Law of Trade Marks and Trade Names. Sweet & Maxwell, 1999.
Pinsonneault & Moscowitz. *The 1995 Annotated Robic-Leger Trademarks Act*. Carswell, 1994.
Robic-Leger. *Canadian Trade-Marks Act Annotated*. 2 volumes, looseleaf. Carswell, 1990.
White. *Selecting and Protecting Trade-Marks 1995*. Canada Practice Guide. Carswell, 1994.

COPYRIGHT AND INDUSTRIAL DESIGN

CIPO. *A Guide to Copyright*. Industry Canada, 1994.
CIPO. *A Guide to Industrial Designs*. Industry Canada, 1994.
Copinger and Skone James On Copyright. Edition 14. Sweet & Maxwell, 1998.
Fox. *The Canadian Law of Copyright and Industrial Designs*. Carswell, 1967.
Hughes on Copyright and Industrial Design. Looseleaf. Butterworths, 1984.
Kratz. *Canadian Intellectual Property Law*. Carswell, 1998.
Kratz. *Protecting Copyright and Industrial Design*. 2nd edition. Canada Practice Guide. Carswell, 1999.
Robic-Leger. *Annotated Canadian Copyright Act*. 2 volumes, looseleaf. Carswell, 1992.
Tamaro. *The 1999 Annotated Copyright Act*. Carswell, 1998.

Index